I, Middle-Aged Man

By: Mike Sprouse

© Mike Sprouse

Photo taken by the Author in Old Saybrook, Connecticut, USA.

*

Dedication

To my parents and stepparents. In a lot of different ways, you all helped me make it here.

To Adrienne, the rest of my family and my children Christian, Ruby and Vivian. I love you and thank you.

To my fellow middle-aged friends, especially Jason, Brian and Marco.

In loving memory of immediate and extended family members who passed away during the writing of this book: Susanne L. Moliere, David H. Fowler, and John P. Moliere, Jr.

*

The "How"

With a full-time career, a newborn baby boy at home, a relatively new marriage, a new town and community, and a few other major life events that have occurred, the last few years writing this book wasn't easy. I also needed to sleep and have some fun doing the things I enjoy doing! Some days more so than others, the standard I was using to hold myself accountable was all about discipline, commitment and consistency, I suppose.

Middle-aged men, those are words we'll use a lot in this book. When those words are put into action together, they sure can take us a long way in every aspect of our lives. As for me, for well over a year I committed to 20 minutes of writing each day during the week, and sometimes longer on weekends. Each day, without fail, I wrote something even if it turned out to be garbage and had to be edited out later. For those 20 minutes or so, either early in the morning or late at night, I was 100% focused on this book. I found that discipline, in any area of life, is something you can always create or find anew each day. That's what I did.

Truthfully, I thought a lot about what the contents of this book might be for probably a good three years. So, a lot of my writing felt like it was writing itself or "flowing" at least. I drew inspiration from other people, some of whom are quoted or referenced in this book. But a lot of my inspiration came from simple observation, reflection and experience. In that way, the contents of this book are not "clinical" even though there is plenty of data behind some of the key points. Instead, the contents in here are meant to be relatable. As with each of my books, I try and write in layman's terms. I hope you'll consider reading this book almost like you are having a fireside chat with a friend.

I don't use an editor (I never have for any of my books) and therefore even an untrained eye will no doubt find mistakes, I'm sure. But as you'll get to know, I'm not especially bothered by that, nor am I bothered by the people who feel it their mission to correct me. To each their own. I simply hope you enjoy the themes and perspectives in the book and find some useful tidbits that you can take with you.

PART I: The Truths

Every man has two lives.

The second one begins when he realizes he has only one.

*

The Lighthouse

Written: April 7, 2018, Locust Hill, E. Canaan, CT.

Remain standing, steady and majestic.
Solid and unshakeable.
Absorbing turbulent waters that surround.
Shine brilliantly.
Be a beacon of light, welcoming.
Reflect brighter to those who travel closest.
Weather storms, welcome the water. They are gifts.
Use the rocks and earth as your foothold for balance.
Be still and accessible,
Knowing not every boat will find you.
Provide safe harbor for the ones that do.
Remain fundamentally unchanged with the passage of time.
Appreciate the beauty in longevity, be unapologetic about it.
See as much as you can on the horizon.
Bask in sunrises and sunsets.
Watch seaweed and debris be carried away by the tides.
But be a sustainable life force to rare species that want to hang on your sides.
Let the overnight breeze carry yesterday away.
Let the morning breeze usher in today's peace.

*

So much of life is determined by how we handle the things, events and situations that don't go the way we imagine or want.

But no matter what happens, we're never a victim of any circumstance in which we find ourselves.

*

If you can dream - and not make dreams your master;

If you can think - and not make thoughts your aim;

If you can meet with Triumph and Disaster

And treat those two impostors just the same

- Rudyard Kipling

*

A Useful Point of View: Stoic Philosophy

Stoicism takes the position that the wise man, the good man, the philosopher, is a man who lives in accordance with nature. <u>He fears only abdicating his principles and moral responsibility</u>. He is not afraid of pain. He is not afraid of death. He is not afraid of poverty. He is not afraid of any of the vicissitudes of the human condition. His only concern is that he should let himself down, and that he should be less than a complete human being.

*

The Wise Farmer

A wise man and his son lived on a farm just outside of a remote town. They owned one horse.

One morning, the farmer and his son were having breakfast and noticed that the horse was nowhere to be found. It had run away. Everyone from the town heard about it and went to the farm. They all said to the man "it's such horrible news, such a shame that you lost your only horse!"

The farmer replied, "I don't know if it's good news or bad news."

The next day, the man and his son were out baling hay in the fields. Suddenly, their horse appeared in the distance and was galloping back towards the farm... alongside two other wild horses! Now the man and his son had three horses.

Having heard the news, everyone from the town dropped by the farm again and said to the farmer "what great news, you have more horses now. It's a miracle!"

The farmer said, "I don't know if it's good or bad news".

The very next day, the man's son hopped up on the back of one of the new horses. The son was thrown off the horse and was very badly hurt. Everyone from the town came by and said, "what horrible news, it's just terrible, we're so sorry that happened".

The farmer said, "I don't know if it's good news or bad news."

The following week while the son was recuperating from his injuries a government official visited the town and announced that they were taking every able-bodied male of a certain age who resided within the town limits to immediately serve in the military. The son was taken out of consideration for active duty because of his injuries and fragile physical state.

Everyone from the town came by and said "what great news! Your son doesn't have to leave, he can stay home with you on the farm!"

The farmer responded, "Don't you see? I don't know yet if it's good or bad news."

*

Good news, bad news, or I don't know. The lesson of this short story is that if we subscribe to the idea that life's events should not be judged as "good news or bad news", we can never possibly believe that anything is bad news. We also aren't quick to label something as good news either. The only thing we always end up finding out is that whatever our judgment is today could likely be different tomorrow.

The Wise Farmer embraces a steady mind and attitude. Not too high, not too low. He regulates his emotions which allows him to keep going forward without chaos or volatility, knowing that the course of events in life can change suddenly. Sometimes, even the very next day. The Wise Farmer is prepared.

*

"This is the true joy in life, being used for a purpose recognized by yourself as a mighty one. Being a force of nature instead of a feverish, selfish little clod of ailments and grievances, complaining that the world will not devote itself to making you happy. I believe that my life belongs to the whole community and as long as I live, it is my privilege to do for it what I can. I want to be thoroughly used up when I die, for the harder I work, the more I live. I rejoice in life for its own sake. Life is no brief candle to me. It is a sort of splendid torch which I have got hold of for the moment and I want to make it burn as brightly as possible before handing it on to future generations.

– George Bernard Shaw

*

Happiness

"The pursuit of happiness." It's right there in the U.S. Declaration of Independence. From the age at which we learn about important historical documents such as that one, we learn about going after happiness, striving for it, chasing it.

The only problem? We're never taught what happiness means or what it looks like. So, most people chase happiness their entire lives, but never know what to look for or even what it resembles. How can we find something if we don't know what we're looking for? Still, a prevailing belief for lots of folks is that happiness is something that's searched for and then found.

Very few people realize, however, that the pursuit of happiness is something conceived, conjured and fostered from within. When someone says, "go find happiness", the first place to look is inside yourself. There's no universal standard for happiness – not money, cars, objects, or things – because it's different for everyone.

Ironically, a great number of us go through life without knowing true happiness may have already been achieved! It might just be lying dormant inside us. Instead, we might get too busy and too distracted to notice. We might be too obsessed with whatever it is we're chasing. Often, people reach old age and think back on a period or instance in their life and say, "oh yeah, I really <u>did</u> know what happiness was all those years ago based on how I remember feeling. I just didn't recognize it!"

Our mission, middle-aged men, is to understand and achieve the spirit of happiness, contentment, and peace from within. Part of our responsibility is to be an example to others about what happiness can look like even if it's not overly showy, flamboyant, or flashy. Most often, true happiness is none of those things. But in order to do that, we must first know it and then live it.

*

Live Unconditionally, not Transactionally

Provide for lots of people but rely on very few.

Expect nothing from anyone else in return.

If something comes back in return, great.

If not, no big deal. We weren't counting on it.

The spirit of giving and providing for others should never be transactional.

No other person should ever be able to disappoint us, since nothing is ever expected from them in return.

It's therefore impossible for us to feel we got the short end of the stick in any situation.

It becomes far easier to be grateful, too.

*

Flexibility

The world around us demands flexibility. Too often, we're fed a constant diet of rigidity by others, by our professions and by society. Even our bodies, science itself tells us, become more rigid as we age. I'm not only talking about our inability to touch our toes while standing straight up like we could when we were young.

It's called cognitive flexibility, and we lose a lot of it over time.

Cognitive flexibility is a critical function that is defined as the ability to adapt our minds and then our behaviors in response to changes in our environment. It's our ability to think clearly and then switch our actions depending on what a given situation requires. Science has shown that our ability to adapt to new situations and environments declines with age, sometimes quickly. In other words, we can get dropped from a helicopter into the middle of nowhere as a 25-year-old and have a much different cognitive response than we would as a 50-year-old. The 25-year-old might go with the flow and think of it as a challenge. The 50-year-old is more likely to panic.

The region of the brain that handles this type of function performs better with the healthier, vibrant neural responses that a younger man possesses. Still, these types of studies which have been published through the years are favorites among many middle-aged men whose neural responses have, shall we say, faded over time. Why?

Because we get it. We relate to it. We get that we're more stubborn when we're older. We're more set in our own ways. We're more apprehensive about the unknown. We dig our heels in more about anything and everything. We tend to see things as more binary, less nuanced. The world around us, and specifically our version of the world and how we see things, gets smaller and narrower. We're not as open-minded, and maybe a little too quick to call something out as wrong, unjust, bad, mean, or crooked if it doesn't fit into our belief system.

I'm not saying this is how it should be. I'm saying it's true, though.

When we are firmly stuck in our own beliefs, our actions never change or adapt because our minds don't give us the go-ahead to change or adapt. New ideas, new people, new places and new things try to penetrate our world, but we have little time or use for them. Sometimes that's not the worst thing. Sometimes it's limiting, though.

There's a lot we know about the stresses of daily life, and most middle-aged men use close-mindedness or stubbornness as a shield against it all. Of course, it's true that we have less time or mental capacity for bullshit or chasing after people or things that are detrimental to our own health. We don't have to do that anymore, after all.

What cognitive flexibility stresses, though, is a need to hone our ability to switch between tasks, strategies, and mental states sharply. And isn't that what we find we need in middle age that we didn't need all that much of a few decades ago? A different mental sharpness. A different type of edge. Instead of our minds becoming blunt instruments over time, we need them to function as sharp objects. I'd argue we need that even more now than we did years ago.

A whole bunch of factors are working against us, though. How many of us like to have a scotch or a beer after a long day of work, and have done so for many years? There's nothing wrong with it. But alcohol consumption for prolonged periods impacts the prefrontal cortex, which is the part of the brain which helps regulate cognitive flexibility.

What if we live a completely clean lifestyle devoid of any of life's traditional vices? Well, the deck is still stacked against us by virtue of simple aging. Some of us are genetically predisposed to a lower degree of cognitive flexibility than others. No matter how much we try and train our minds, it may never change if our genetic wiring prohibits it.

The irony in considering and then maintaining our own cognitive flexibility is that it requires a fair amount of cognitive stability. We need to have established a sound mind in order to avoid chaotically changing directions or tasks at the drop of a hat. We must train our mind to have some level of focus, or we'll be chasing every new idea, thing or thought that comes our way.

The cognitive stability we need to keep our cognitive flexibility boils down to one word: discernment. Having a discerning mind means maintaining a high level of awareness in knowing when we need to shift, change, move, or react; and when we don't need to react to something at all.

It's a balance, and a constantly changing one, not surprisingly. It means we must continuously refine a new mindset as we go through this phase of our lives. It's not about closing doors completely off; it's about knowing what doors we're required to open and how fast we need to open them. It's knowing what doors we want to open no matter how long it takes, and what doors we simply aren't sure about right now.

But we should also work on being able to touch our toes while standing straight up.

*

Competition

Don't compete with other people anymore. Compete with the man in the mirror. Compete against what we think we're capable of and what our capacity is. Don't stop to contemplate or question whether our lives have peaked or hit their ceiling.

They haven't.

*

You deserve the prosperity that you've earned.

*

Author's Meditation: About Middle Age

What exactly does it mean to be "middle-aged"?

Typically, it means we're 40-65 years old, though most people often consider that middle age really begins in one's late 40's and lasts up until retirement age. It's the period in our lives after young adulthood and before what's generally considered old age.

Middle age is often believed to accompany feelings of nostalgia, sadness, boredom, and lack of fulfillment to name just a few. Left unchecked or if we're unaware of it, we can easily see how these conditions might be true. Our bodies start to naturally slow down and there are visible, physical signs of aging. Muscle mass starts to erode, sex drive and vitality drops for most of us, we become more sensitive to foods and changes to our diet and our exercise regimen decreases. As a result, we start to "magically" accumulate greater fat levels. Plus, there are those unavoidable wrinkles we start to see while shaving each morning in the mirror.

Does any of this sound familiar?

While most of these physical symptoms emerge, our minds are left to wonder what the hell is happening. Where did that vibrant young 25-year-old man go? How did the myriad challenges we now face emerge so suddenly (it seems) at this stage of our lives? Some challenges are physical like not being able to touch our toes. But what about all these mental, financial, personal and professional ones too?

We'll get into this more later, but when I was 43, I had some massive challenges and fought like no one's ever fought before just to get into middle age. What was the prize for that?

Well, there were only a handful of people who really believed in me. None of the "good" I had done in my life up until that point, none of the things I felt so good about achieving once upon a time, were revered much less remembered. Some prize! Welcome to middle age!

I recall thinking, and to this day somewhat still believe, that maybe five people in the world thought I could come back and be competent much less good at anything personally or professionally again. The down periods, the struggles, seemed to have a big spotlight on them, as if I was done, kaput, over the hill, written off.

Dead before I was buried.

Most people really don't like to see someone at their lowest, lowest point, because it's ugly. The flip side, which is an absolute truth, is most people really don't like to see someone at their absolute highest point either.

The people that celebrate our highest level, our best selves, are <u>our</u> people. That's our tribe. The ones who see our good no matter what, unconditionally. Sometimes those people are hard to find. If we can't find them, then we must be our own one-person tribe in that regard.

So, to the surprise of some and the deep despair of a few, I did in fact make it to middle age. In fact, I've thrived, which is to say that I've become whole on the inside. That's my gauge. Through all those life experiences, I was sure entering middle age would be a cause for celebration, though. I made it!

Until I found that practically every man in our age bracket struggles with lots of the same emotions I did. We realize that nothing's permanent. Experiences and memories are fleeting. We experience pain and heartbreak. We're tired more often. We fight against age as opposed to welcoming it. Our aches and pains start adding up. We can't do things physically we once did and that plays on us mentally.

Yet, there might be so much more left to go, or so we hope. So, here's the good stuff. Our perspectives are now well-rooted in our <u>own</u> experiences versus having to listen to someone else's opinion telling us how they see things or how things are going to be. We know the truth from what <u>we</u> see and experience, not from what we're told by anyone else.

Plus, we see through bullshit a lot easier because we have wisdom. We have more tolerance and empathy for some people, like people who push themselves through challenges or jump into a worthy endeavor or set a high bar for success for themselves. After all, we know how tough life can be.

On the flip side, we might have a lot less tolerance for some people, like people who are toxic, destructive, back-stabbing, manipulative, angry, or just plain mean. We can wish them well and still discern not to waste our precious cognitive stability on them!

In either case, we have a lot of life experience at this point, right now, to be able to tell the difference. This fact immediately qualifies us to be in the middle-aged club. We've heard a lot, seen a lot, and gone through a lot. Some of what we've heard, seen and experienced has been great and some of it hasn't lived up to our expectations. Roll it all up, and we're here, right now, currently, without a definitive roadmap of what the rest of middle age and old age look like. If we're looking for one, we won't find it. If we think we have one, it will change. Things almost never go exactly according to plan, just ask The Wise Farmer. Flexibility will be key. Adaptability will be key.

But our <u>attitude</u> and therefore our perspectives will be the biggest keys to a prosperous life.

*

Life's Secrets

We have made it this far in life. Take a second and feel some pride in that. Pause for just a minute and give yourself a little bit of a pat on the shoulder. Not too hard or you might injure something.

Now, here's a secret: it's not about us, or acting with the sole intent of benefiting ourselves, anymore. It's about what we can provide other people with, and how we're able to elevate those around us. It takes a while sometimes for our approach to develop. But when it does, the emotional benefits we earn from this period of our lives, starting now and going forward, are far greater than any we've earned from the work we've done with ourselves as the focal point up until now.

Here's another more exciting secret: it doesn't mean we can't still dream more dreams and live more of our lives on our terms. That mindset can and should exist alongside providing for others, not despite it. We can reset our standards about what is and isn't acceptable for us. It doesn't mean we expect people to live up to these standards (remember, expect nothing from anyone). It means we're giving others the tools, knowledge and resources to try. Open doors for people and give them the means to go through them.

Lastly: there's a prevailing notion out there that we can't have it all in life. We can. We don't think we can. But we can. Personally, or professionally, we think that our ship may have left the harbor by now. That we've missed our shots. But no. We can earn everything we want. Nothing and no one are stopping us, except us.

*

If someone or something is trying to kick you in the ass, it means you're in front. Go faster and keep blazing.

*

What Other People Think

Why do we care what people think about us? Because for some, it's natural. It's also been wired into us over decades going back to when we were kids. But why does it matter now? Life isn't a popularity contest. Even the most beloved people in history still had a high number of people who disliked them. The most-liked person we can think of right this minute has someone who doesn't like them. So, why do we care?

A much better question for us, though, is this: why do we care more about what other people think about us than what we think about us?

Because that's often true. We get taught early in our lives to try and go above and beyond for other people in the interest of service, common good, decency and being a productive member of society. None of us ever get taught with the same depth about how to care for ourselves, our mind, our well-being and our attitude. Was there ever a class we took on self-confidence? Not likely for any of us. We must learn all that on the fly, with the embarrassment of being labeled as potentially selfish if the scales tip too far.

It's no wonder then that we become frazzled or disillusioned when people slight us. We take it as a personal indictment even if it's not personal. Sometimes, we feel let down by other people criticizing us, people supposedly close to us. We feel betrayed sometimes. We feel constrained. We feel disrespected by specific speech and language used towards us. We get talked down to, judged, put under a microscope, questioned. Some days, it can seem to us like a Salesclerk at a store is the nicest person on the planet, much more so than our own loved ones.

All of these are emotions that we, as middle-aged men, ideally should be able to block out or just easily move past. "Should be able to" is the operative phrase. Society tells us that at this stage of our lives, we should just easily be able to let this stuff go. When we can't, our instincts are to blame others or the world around us as the cause of our discontent or hurt feelings.

But that's never it. It's never someone else's fault for how we choose to interpret anything said or done to us. We're never victims, ever. It's no one's obligation to feel sorry for us, or to watch out for our own best interests, or to be extra nice to us. It's our responsibility to measure our response to what's happening around us, specifically other people's energies, and then choose how to react. Sometimes we get pissed off, but holding onto that for too long, for any middle-aged man, isn't very efficient.

There's another word: efficient. One of the goals for us in middle age is efficiency. It's going through life with the least possible drama and unnecessary baggage. We know that there will be speed bumps, sometimes big ones along the way, which is why efficiency in life is so important for us. No matter what, we still need to move forward skillfully, adeptly and righteously. The goal is to move through life with the utmost efficiency and no dead weight attached to us like negative emotions, constantly revisited trauma, laziness, drama, gaslighting, and the wrong people.

Taking things too personally when we know better truly slows down our efficiency in life more than anything.

*

If you focus on the obstacles in front of you, all you will ever see are the obstacles in front of you.

If you focus on a path through or around the obstacles, all you will see is opportunity.

*

What is Success?

The short answer? Self-actualization. We'll get to that.

But what this book will <u>not</u> tell middle-aged men to do? "Follow your passion".

That is old and tired wisdom, and it's just not great or practical advice either. It's bullshit when using it as a North Star for success. Ask any number of fulfilled, self-actualized or successful people how they've found success in their lives, and they wouldn't tell us they simply "followed their passion" either. It's more than that. We can be passionate about something and really stink at it. Then, the more we follow it, we find out it leads nowhere fast in the best case, and nowhere slow in the worst case. This is why people don't just follow their passions in life without any aptitude for them.

Instead, it's in some ways the opposite approach that many follow to success. Find out and be honest with ourselves about what we're good at, with a chance at becoming great at, and work at it. Everyone has something, and the key is finding it anew or finding it again. What could we be great at with a little bit of work? Answer that question, and we put ourselves at the start of a journey.

It's our dedication in working on what we're good at that then ignites our passion. Then, when little bits of success start coming, the passion builds even greater. The process of work and fine-tuning our craft becomes passion in and of itself. Successful outcomes then simply become byproducts of the work we've done. Our craft, which started out as something we liked and were good at, is something that becomes one of our great passions in life with the results to with it. Great passions are therefore built over a rather lengthy process. A process that isn't too late to for us to start. We're not too old.

The hang-up is that few of us learn how to build passions based on what we're good at. We follow the wrong approach way too late in life for most of us to do anything about.

The best athletes, inventors, and businesspeople didn't wake up one day and say, "I'm passionate about this thing, sport or hobby even though I suck at it." More likely, they knew early on that they had a specific skill or talent. Perhaps a talent in basketball, or they were fast, or they understood technology extremely well, or they could hit the high notes in music class, or they were super-quick at calculating numbers, or they were incredibly gifted creatively without even trying it seemed. Then, they worked on it. They kept doing it repeatedly.

Think back to when you first realized you were good at something. Generally, it meant you had some affinity for it too. Too often, especially later in life, we stray from the very things we're good at and could be great at, and therefore don't maximize the talents we have to their fullest. We give too few of our talents the patience and space to be able to blossom into passions.

Besides, what we're good at, we probably enjoy. It's fun to be good at something. What we enjoy, we don't mind doing a million times repetitively. When we do something a million times repetitively, we become a Master of it. As we go through the process of mastery, passion builds. When we master something, we have a high chance for success.

What goes into the process of mastery? It means going through things like failure, challenges, little successes, failure again, sacrifices, discipline and commitment. And, likely, repeating each of these a few times. It also involves tuning out all the naysayers, and there will be a bunch of them. The point is: it's not too late to develop your skills into passions, and not too late to earn the success you deserve.

*

Author's Meditation on "The Why"

In a busy man's life, especially a middle-aged man's life, there are very few moments of genuine peace. I have a fulltime career and have <u>developed</u> a passion over the last several years for writing books. Finding moments of peace is a challenge, but I had to in order to find my "why".

If any of my perspectives can help someone or give them a glimpse of a different perspective or entertain them, those are among my goals. Those things help fuel my passion. It's my "why". If someone writes books looking to get rich or famous as the root of their passion, they'll be sorely disappointed in most cases. It took the author of one of my favorite books, Paulo Coelho, decades after he initially wrote *The Alchemist* to even get noticed by more than a handful of people. Getting rich or famous is not the "why" behind a good author's purpose. After all, there are a lot of easier ways to get rich!

My first book, *The Greatness Gap*, was written almost 15 years prior to this one. At the time, I still remember when I saw a particular relative from my ex's family who fashioned himself as a savvy lawyer and businessman. He would always open our conversations by asking, "so, how many books have you sold?" This was before he even said hello to me.

I always felt like saying "I'll sell a lot more when I stop listening to your bullshit." I was in my 30's then, and not yet middle aged, so I didn't. Instead, I was polite. I didn't realize then that I should have told him to kick rocks and had the full authority to do so. I had a long-term approach to my process, not a short-term money-grabbing one. It was clear his "why" and my "why" were never even in the same universe. (My "why" was better in the long run by the way.)

No, the "why" of writing for me and most authors is because we have something to say, and we think other people might share some of our same thoughts. As writers we're able to <u>relate</u> to people or find common ground based on shared experiences or perspectives. How does one even know unless we put pen to paper and try? In my case, how would I know if we had shared experiences if I couldn't even stop long enough to ponder what being a middle-aged man really means? How could I relate to anyone if I couldn't put together a collection of thoughts to start a dialogue from?

For us middle-aged men, there is very little time for true reflection in our lives. Writing this book has been my 20+ minutes of daily solitude and reflection. I've found this struggle for time to be true for lots of us, though.

You see, parts of my story are no different than yours probably. Even if you and I have pursued paths in life that are completely different from one another, there are still similarities. There are some analogous events, trains of thought, and parallels in our journeys. While the details of what I've done might not be identical to yours, the perspective and context could very well be. I can say confidently that I bet the physical and emotional challenges we face are similar, too. The "why" of my writing, I suppose, is to release all of that into the wild and discuss it.

I've conferred with hundreds of men above the age of 40 over the course of the last decade in various lines of work I've done. I've worked at a ski resort among dozens of middle-aged guys with the same things on our minds. I've worked in addiction treatment as a counselor which was a world full of middle-aged guys with real problems like mine. I've worked in large corporations and seen men in their prime and well-past their prime struggle for meaning and purpose. I lived at and worked on a farm for years, where I was embedded with rural middle-agers and how they see the world. I worked for a very well-known men's entertainment brand – with the moniker "Entertainment for Men" - for five years. I suppose I found out along the way in my career the unique trains of thought that lots of us share is sometimes found in totally different walks of life or lines of work. There's commonality in more places than you'd ever realize.

We collectively have demands placed on us – by a spouse, a family member, fans, friends, kids, grandkids or society at large – that are unique. We're looked at differently, sometimes with reverence, other times with scorn or contempt. I often joke with people that literally no employer wants to hire a middle-aged man. It used to be that we were entering our prime!

Nope, not now it seems. Most employers either want people younger and cheaper, or older with just a few years left until retirement who can be the adult in the room. Same thing if you're single as a middle-aged guy. For some people, you're too old with too much baggage to date; for others, you're too young to be in your easy-going golden years. In an instant it seems, we look up and see that we still have things we're figuring out while still catering to other people's needs and struggling to take care of our own needs.

That last part is important. Think about it: how much time do we really spend taking stock of our lives and taking care of our well-being outside of work responsibilities, career, financial obligations, caring for family, or sleeping a little bit if we're lucky?

There's always something pulling us in one direction or the other, and often the forces seem to pull us in ways that we don't deep down really want to go. When that happens, it's a great time to pause and reflect on our "why". Long gone are those childhood dreams you once dreamt of, most likely. Long gone are those entirely free weekends of sleeping past 8AM or going golfing for entire days or weekends. Even our past achievements, successes or things we're proud of are probably distant memories at this point. Somewhere deep in our psyche, we can sort of remember experiences in our early 20's or 30's that seemed to us at the time like the biggest things ever to happen to anyone in the entire world!

Yet now, we're in this fuzzy area between living our lives with youth and vitality, and retirement and death. And in fact, many of our family and friends have been in that latter category as of late, I'm sure.

So, now what?

*

"Beware of overconcern for money, or position, or glory. Someday you will meet a man who cares for none of these things. Then you will know how poor you are."

-   Rudyard Kipling

*

Our Best

There is a truth that has been kept a secret from a lot of us for a long time. The part that <u>isn't</u> a secret is that the better we are, the better it is for our families, spouse, and kids. Hopefully you have the support you need within that triad to be your best.

The part that is a secret typically refers to people around us who are outside of our close-knit group. It's that the better we are – the professional us, the inner us, the competitive us, the <u>complete</u> us – the more other people may not like it. If we take anything from this book and improve ourselves from it, it means we're taking aspects of our lives into our own hands (thereby taking something away from someone else, potentially, if they control those aspects of our lives). It's a risk we'll have to weigh. Those friends, partners, spouses, and family members who truly want to see us as the best version of ourselves will cheer us on. Some other people simply won't or will do so begrudgingly while dishing out guilt. Or they'll fake it.

That's one easy way to take inventory of the people we should spend more of our valuable time with: they're the ones cheering us on when we're doing our best, not just when there's something in it for them when we're at our worst.

How do we take more control of ourselves and our minds, thoughts, and emotions? As we journey through middle age and embrace some renewed perspectives, we will inevitably create a gap. A gap between us and people who may have felt they controlled us or got a lot of our time or could manipulate our mind or tell us how to think or act.

Middle-aged men, we're not doing that anymore, and there are consequences. A rule of thumb to remember: the higher we vibe, the smaller our tribe.

Putting it this way doesn't mean we don't care about other people. In fact, we place a greater emphasis on embracing close, genuine friendships and kinship. It's about being honest about who those people are. There will be people who won't be able to meet the standard we set for ourselves in certain aspects of our lives. Once we determine that, there will be an inevitable division.

The process of becoming our best selves makes every single person we encounter take their own inventory. Very few people are willing to honestly do that. People who maybe aren't their best selves see you as a target to figuratively chop at the knees. Maybe jealous. Maybe envious. Maybe secretly not wanting you to be as good, as peaceful, as free, as you are becoming.

But we're middle-aged men, not kids or young adults. Again, why would we listen to people who want to criticize us, belittle us, and drag us down?

What we do from here forward as middle-aged men is our life's work. So, it's a big deal. People who aren't as enlightened as we aim to be can drag us down faster than we can bring them up. We need to be aware of that. The concepts we discuss here are tough and against the grain. In a world of people wanting "more", others naturally will want what we have once they see us at our best. Let's share the best of ourselves, but just be a little bit more discerning about who we share it with is all.

*

Well-being is realized by taking lots of small steps, but it is truly no small thing.

*

The Meaning of Life

In recent years, we might have wondered what it's all meant up until now and even more importantly what it could possibly mean as we navigate this part of our journey. Maybe we've accomplished a ridiculous amount and had a successful career. Maybe we haven't done anything yet. Maybe we have millions of adoring fans. Maybe we have none. Maybe we have a family we're proud of. Maybe we had a family that fractured for whatever reason. Maybe we have a lot of people who dislike us. Maybe we've made millions of dollars. Maybe we've lost it all and went bankrupt. Maybe we've traveled all over the world, and maybe we never left our hometown.

Regardless of where we've been and what we've done, we're all going through similar confusing thoughts and experiences. We're bridging the gap between our supposed "prime" and the "Back Nine of life" to reference a golf term.

Middle-age-ness forces us to answer the question, though, doesn't it? The meaning of life question. What exactly is life's meaning?

The answer is that there is no answer, because it is whatever we decide it to be at any given moment. It's also highly likely that it can and will change frequently. How each of us answers the question is deeply personal and unique. The meaning of life is something we all get to choose and have the right to alter along the way.

Which brings us back to those moments of quiet, calm and peace. We can use these fleeting moments of peace wisely. It's in these moments that we can define the answer to the meaning of life question for ourselves, since we're the only ones who can answer it. No guru, doctor, or motivational speaker can answer it for us.

Some of us used to fight this whole notion with everything we had. There had to be one universal meaning, we thought. There had to be a secret that only the truly transformational or spiritually transcendent beings knew. We had to know the secret, had to find the answer.

No. If you've been searching high and low for a universal answer that applies to all of us, you're misguided. The meaning of life is whatever we choose it to be, and to truly manifest it we must decide it and then act with total conviction towards it. There are no half measures when it comes to what we believe is the meaning behind it all. It's ours to decide and act upon.

You maybe have heard many of these so-called experts, gurus and spiritual teachers, claim that "life is all about suffering", or even more simply that "life's meaning is suffering", or something like that.

That is such a crock of shit. Certainly, the meaning of life doesn't have anything to do with suffering. After all, suffering happens to everyone. It's not unique. It's a byproduct of life. It's a part of life that we simply must deal with. It's not the meaning behind it all.

Instead, we place our mind and energy on what we believe is important and significant at a point in time, and then follow it until there's nothing more left to follow. Then, rinse and repeat. Over and over, maybe a half-dozen times, the deeper meaning of our lives will change. No matter how many times it changes, the common thread is we get to choose it and then derive the degree of meaning we take from it.

Part of our lives at this midpoint is about understanding things that could cause us to suffer emotionally and then take active measures to either counteract them or rise above them. Some of us have mastered this skill and some of us are still in the process of mastering it. Because life's a continual, constant test of regulating emotions, we can and should come back to the things in which we derive most meaning. The areas of life that are most special and dear to us. The areas that align with our true purpose. The areas that bring us joy, bring us peace.

It seems so simple now, but unfortunately most of us spend the early part of our life doing everything possible to pass every test imaginable from physical to societal. As if that were the meaning: to prove ourselves to someone else. We feel the need to prove ourselves to everyone else in the world up to a certain age.

Then, we finally reach a point where we understand it was never about proving anything to anyone else. It was about proving everything to ourselves. We realize the tests we tried to pass, at everyone else's urging in our younger days, don't harvest fruit for us any longer. They're in a sense, meaningless.

Maybe not totally, though. Perhaps all those tests we passed to this point in our lives were so that we can stand firmly, strongly and powerfully here now and wherever the rest of our lives take us. Every test we passed had some type of purpose even if they seem irrelevant now.

This next part is special, though.

At some point in middle age, we won't even feel the need to prove ourselves to ourselves. We'll know who we are, what we're capable of and feel good about it. The meaning of our lives will be almost predestined or preordained. We won't search for it, we won't stress over it, and we won't have to struggle to find it. It doesn't mean we stop trying or stop living! It just means we know what we have inside of us, and the meaning behind things seems like an afterthought.

Other people – family members, friends, colleagues, strangers - might want to extract more and more out of us like they could when we were younger. But we reach a point where we're good. We're not as malleable anymore. We're not easily manipulated. We're finished products at our core. At some point, the timing of which is decided upon by each person individually, we get to lean into that and take some joy – and yes, meaning – from the finished products we're becoming.

*

There are no problems in any middle-aged man's life.

Only choices.

*

What's Your "More"?

When we hit middle age, it's natural to think about whether we have lived up to our potential. It's easy to fall into a thought pattern of whether we wasted precious years or missed any opportunities along the way. One of the things we've asked ourselves is: was I meant for <u>more</u>? More success, more impact, more joy, more love, more money, more passion, more thrills, more travel, or more meaningful pursuits?

What's your "more"?

If we're human, we're constantly looking for, or are aware of, the possibility of there being something more. We go looking for more in a variety of possible different places: a church, a bar, a yoga studio, on top of a mountain, in front of a television, or sitting outside on the porch in our favorite chair. We ponder it all and consider "what do I do now?" or "is it too late for me?" or "is this really what I made of my life so far?" or "is THIS all there is for me?"

It's not too late for almost anything to change regardless of how old or healthy we are. Even if we're chronically ill, the road hasn't been closed yet. Along the way up until now, it's natural for us to stop dreaming, stop taking calculated risks, and stop feeling like we're moving forward with any type of excitement or momentum. It's easy to forget all those times when we were younger and we would just do something, anything, without really worrying about the outcome or the risks. We feared a lot less than we do today.

So, where did that person go? The one who was always motivated by going after "more"?

Well, that person and persona never really left. For most of us, we spend a good chunk of our lives seeking to find something that we have either lost or never found. This seeking becomes intensified in middle age when we realize that we have only one physical life, and it's ours to do whatever we want with. Inevitably, we start to really question whether we have reached the fullest potential of our capacity. We wonder if we have become self-actualized.

Make no mistake about what it means to be a self-actualized person. Very simply, self-actualized people believe that they <u>must</u> be what they <u>can</u> be.

But isn't it too late for all that? No. A good many of us find the process of self-actualizing to be a main goal and purpose of middle age. In fact, an even higher goal for some people is self-transcendence, or going <u>beyond</u> what we previously thought our capacity could be. It's the very top level of Abraham Maslow's pyramid, for those familiar with it. It's also why you see a lot of middle-aged men atop Mount Everest.

They simply must figuratively (and then literally) climb to the summit of their physical and emotional capabilities, to reach rarefied air beyond their wildest dreams.

It's healthy to subscribe to the theory that it's not too late for us to climb our own metaphorical Everest, however we define that for ourselves. What we often lack is the time, focus, presence of mind and discipline to manifest what we think about. Lots of us talk ourselves out of it too, don't we? Apprehension and fear get in the way. Or such-and-such will take too much time, or too much energy, or too much risk, or too much sacrifice.

But a wise man once put it the following way. The questions we always need to ask and then answer for ourselves are: 1) what do we want? and 2) what price are we willing to pay to get it?

Then, you have your "more".

*

Some More Truths

We've heard the saying that with age comes wisdom. Sometimes, it takes a lifetime for us to learn lessons that we could have acted upon earlier to improve the quality of our lives. Woulda, coulda, shoulda, right? But it's not too late to do anything or be anyone you want to be, though, if we level with ourselves. Let's talk about some more truths and start with one from Socrates:

1) <u>Know thyself</u>. A life that is truly examined – not by others, but by oneself – is a life with deeper meaning and greater understanding. By knowing ourselves better than anyone else can, we more definitively know our unique purpose. We know our tendencies in certain situations. We know our reactions to things. In this truth, it's not about changing; it's about <u>understanding</u> and <u>accepting</u>. Though they can sometimes assist you, therapists, spouses, parents and children shouldn't be telling us who we are now. We should know who we are and what we're all about. So, trust is important, and specifically trusting our most basic instincts going forward. It's about knowing that if we're here now, we're survivors and have a lifetime's worth of wisdom. We must

truly believe it, though, and believe that everything that encompassing "us" is enough.

2) Embrace friendships. Sometimes, we think we don't "need" friends. We don't need others to bond with or talk about life with. But the truth is that we all need meaningful social interactions. If we're not great at making new friends, we can continue to cultivate old ones. We never forget the importance of friendships that are truly equal and not transactional. Quality friendships over quantity. We can focus on the ones that have mutual respect, genuine feelings of well-being for each other, and even admiration. It's okay to admire others and the lives they've worked hard to build, if the relationship is never too one-sided.

There is one caveat to embracing friendships. The stereotypical male ego can get a little too edgy or territorial sometimes. So, we make sure there is a balance to that competitive push and pull in our friendships. We make sure there is a foundation of respect in place.

3) Everything in life is impermanent. Get to know the concept of impermanence. We're mortal. Our time will be up on this earth someday. Some relationships stand the test of a very long time, but even they end someday. Our health and vitality aren't forever. Nothing in our life is as permanent as we think it is if we really stop to think. For this reason, we embrace the fleeting nature of people, places and things. We appreciate

and celebrate everything at every chance. We fill our hearts with gratitude that with each new day we're getting a "+1".

An interesting thing happens when we do all this: we begin to let go of things that no longer serve us. In essence, we don't hang onto things for too long since whatever it is we're hanging onto will not be around forever anyway. We keep what we want and need.

4) <u>Strive for some balance</u> (with a caveat). Balance is a word that gets tossed around a lot, and most people take it to mean "well-rounded." This is something that we middle-aged men, especially, struggle with. We try to do it all. Often, we put our mental and physical health on the back burner for a day, week or months. People tell us that our lives are out of balance. But we're just trying to do lots of things well simultaneously. And that's okay.

The caveat to balance comes in this: to be truly exceptional or to maximize our own potential at anything, it decidedly takes a <u>lack</u> of balance in order to make that happen. It takes total commitment and total discipline to become great at anything. People pursuing excellence tend to leave balance in their lives behind in favor of their pursuit sometimes at all costs. Nobody ever scolded Michael Jordan for having a lack of work/life balance! Because sometimes that's what it takes, and you must do what it takes even if it puts you off balance for a bit of time.

5) <u>Self-care is important</u>. Some of us put lots of other people first. We forget about the very things that our parents stressed to us, and that we likely have stressed to our children: the importance of sleep and proper rest. The importance of grooming, including oral care, skin care, and hair care if we're lucky enough to still have some. The importance of physical fitness. The importance of vitality and sexual health. Finally, the importance of emotional well-being perhaps through deep breathing, yoga, meditation, or just simply having a little bit of time each day for quiet reflection. If we fail to practice self-care, there's no possible path to becoming self-actualized or even the best version of ourselves. It's that simple.

*

One of the great mysteries of life that a middle-aged man must solve for himself is determining what is truly up to him and what is not up to him.

With one, he must act with decisiveness, conviction and authority.

With the other, he must exercise restraint, calm and confidence in knowing that his <u>inaction</u> is indeed the right course of action.

*

Our Health

We don't hear a ton about mental health issues facing middle-aged men these days. We hear and see a whole lot of advertisements for fat-burning supplements, testosterone boosters, or the next great hair replacement treatments. These aren't the real <u>health</u> issues we're referring to, though. It's the ones middle-aged men in particular face that none of us really want to talk about all that much.

Before we get to them, let's all be each other's advocates in this, shall we? We face unique challenges as we age, don't let anyone tell you differently. Put aside the narrative you hear from some people about "men being so lucky" and "men aging gracefully, it's so not fair."

That narrative, too, is a crock of shit. The truth is that we are in somewhat of an unspoken crisis, and it's not getting better. Some of it is our own doing, though.

Let's start with life expectancy. As of the early 2020's, it is <u>six</u> years shorter for men compared to women. That gap is the largest it's been since the 1980's.

Men, typically, have the worst health outcomes for the things that are most likely to be lethal. Covid-19? The death rate was 60% higher for men at the height of it. Diabetes? Historically, 60% higher for men as well. Cancer mortality rate? 40% higher for men. The rate of suicide? Four times higher in men.

72% of motor vehicle fatalities happen to men. Pedestrian, motorcycle and bicycling deaths are heavily skewed towards men, 85% according to the same early 2020's statistics.

Underneath these statistics, we need to level with each other about the "why". Because the facts show that we also probably don't know how to prioritize our health very well. And that's on us.

One area of research shows that women do a far better job of utilizing preventative care than men do. Men vastly underutilize available healthcare, as a rule, while women mainly do it correctly – how we're all supposed to do it - tempering a better balance between preventative and reactionary care. Physician visit rates are 40% higher for women. The top reasons men visit their doctors are "stamina", sexual health and erectile dysfunction.

Of course.

Those are important, but why do we do this to ourselves? Men are largely taught as boys to not complain about their ailments and even hide them. Cultural expectations generally hold that men should remain unbothered, or at least give off that impression, about whatever bugs us. What do you think that leads to?

Depression. The silent killer for middle-aged men. "Put on a brave face", the familiar narrative goes. That's all well and good, but depression is a real thing for us. Feelings of entrapment, our needs not being met, like our life is an endless cycle, and that our purpose has fluttered away over the years are all prevailing feelings we may have. Men are much less likely to proactively go to therapy than women, data shows, and so we just keep quiet. That's okay if you have your own internal mechanisms on how to cope with frustration and depressive feelings. It's not okay if you're really struggling and need help.

One area we do get right as a group is with prostate health. We're aware of it and generally are better educated in prostate health than other areas of men's healthcare. We're certainly better educated than our parents and grandparents were. Still, awareness could be better. There are no pink ribbons or symbolic reminders in society of any men's health issue. There's no "awareness" month to speak of currently. So, while we do a good job in one or two areas related to men's health, it often comes at the expense of other things like cardiac care or mental health.

Gentlemen, this is a wake-up call. Healthcare is key. Longevity (not only in the bedroom) is key. It's not only important for us but for the countless loved ones that we impact every day. Our families. Our friends. It can all vanish in a second. So, why not cherish our time here and make something out of it and give ourselves as much time as possible to do what we want to do in this life?

There are many well-researched behavioral, biological, and social factors that put our group at a high-risk health-wise. The data is out there if we need to read for ourselves. What we should understand, though, is that men – by the time middle age rolls around – are by far the <u>bigger drain on society</u> compared to women from a healthcare perspective. Chew on that for a minute. After the age of 65, men <u>cost</u> the healthcare system in the U.S. 30% more than women do.

Why aren't we talking about our health more? The data shows we are in a real health crisis by the time we get to middle age, and maybe before that, and it's not improving.

Another thing we should consider is this: we're talking about all kinds of things – emotions, feelings, situations, perspectives – in this book, and talking about how to deal, cope, actualize and transcend the path we've established so far in life. All the great thinking and great ideas don't mean much if you're not around to put them into action. So, this is a call to action. Let's think about our bodies as our temples again. Treat them and regard them with as much importance as we did when we were 17 years old, back when we were trying to impress people. Throw away the vanity aspect of it because we don't need it now, but let's have that same level of reverence for our bodies now that we once did.

By the time we reach middle age, we've probably done quite a bit of sitting in chairs. Our backs are tied up in knots. Our hamstrings are tight. Our range of motion from our shoulders, hips and ankles is up to 40% less than it was when we were in our 20's. 40%!

No, men don't age gracefully at all. We might be able to hide it well, but a lot of us are shadows of our old selves physically.

It's time to stand up and do something, and a great place to start is a full-body flexibility routine. Day one of this will suck. The first few days will suck. The obvious focal points are the shoulders, back, hips, quadriceps, hamstrings, calves and neck. The less obvious focal points are the forearms, wrists, ankles, feet (yes, feet), and triceps. We won't even worry about our biceps anymore. Our triceps take up 2/3 of our arm's muscle mass anyway.

Of course, we lose our core and ab strength as we age. Ironically, this is a main cause of our lower back problems. As we make strides in our flexibility routine, we'll throw in a few crunches to keep our guts strong. It will help our backs.

As for our minds, we're working on them. They will always be beautifully complex works in progress. Understand that the better care we take of our bodies, our minds will follow. Do a brisk workout, work up a sweat and get out of breath and see how we feel ten minutes later. The endorphin rush will last us an entire day, and our moods will naturally improve. Our moods are key ingredients to everything we think about and therefore manifest.

*

Bias

I possess a terrible bias. It is a terrible bias that I never used to have, but I now hold onto dearly. It is not a bias towards or against any race, creed, political party, nationality, religion, sexual orientation, gender identification or socioeconomic class.

It is a bias towards people who hold self-respect, kindness, appreciation, and gratitude as their foremost virtues. This is a bias I don't compromise.

For you see, there was a period in my life when I attracted energies and auras that were the opposite of those virtues. Not only did I attract them, but I was also attracted to them. As part of my own journey of self-actualizing, I understood that in order to be my best I cannot surround myself with anyone who doesn't possess these core principles.

There are some days, when me, you, and everyone isn't their most kind or gracious or appreciative. Sometimes, we just plain make wrong decisions in our personal lives or professional careers. But I'm talking about hanging around people with a pattern of destructive behavior exhibited over a long period of time, and therefore a well-established track record.

Some biases are healthy, especially as they relate to our emotional well-being. How often have we, as middle-aged men, put up with behavior for far too long that is otherwise unacceptable? How often have we given chance after chance to people who simply haven't earned it? How often have we drifted away from people who are too kind, or too generous, or too respectful?

Likely, the answers are "often". Or at least, "too often." Let's think about our biases. Think about the situations or people we're drawn to through guilt, pressure or coercion, or because we feel we must, or because someone else is forcing our hand. Because in those situations, we're going against our own natural biases and therefore putting suffering in play for ourselves. This is why I commit to holding to these very distinct biases that I know for sure I'm guilty of holding.

*

Today is the tomorrow we were worried about yesterday.

Fear

It's true that a source of many people's anxiety, depression, and mental anguish boils down to fear. It has been well-documented through countless research studies that fear causes any number of negative outcomes and derivative behaviors in people.

Fear is about the future, or that which hasn't happened yet. Only on occasion do we have reason to fear something that is already in the past. We mainly fear things about to happen or that will happen days, weeks or months ahead of time. The anticipation of a big event, presentation, encounter or that which is unknown is enough to get us all tied up in knots.

Because that's what fear is all about. The unknown. Uncertainty. When a specific outcome is out of our control.

The irony is that in middle age, when so much is already <u>behind</u> us and less is ahead of us, our fear levels increase. In essence, with experiences, mistakes and successes piling up from our past and a shorter time ahead of us in the future, our fears and anxieties pile up more. We live our daily lives taking fewer and fewer risks and becoming more afraid of the unknown. Maybe it's because we can sense that the clock is ticking more now than it was 30 years ago.

One reason why might be because our mortality comes into clearer focus. The drumbeat becomes louder when we start to lose people around us that we care about. In the last few years, we've likely had numerous people pass away including close childhood friends, mentors, family members and colleagues.

When people our age or younger start passing away or leaving this physical world, it hits different now for us. We fear that we might be next. One gentleman I know of passed away in the middle of a walk one day. His heart just stopped beating and he collapsed and couldn't be revived. Otherwise, he was known to be in very good health. He was 46 years old.

What the heck do we say about something like that? Other examples, I'm sure, about friends and loved ones come into focus the more we think about them. We think "one day someone is here, the next they're not. Is my time coming? Do I prepare or how do I prepare?"

With questions like these that truly have no right answers, the elements of fear start to creep into our minds. We don't know what's ahead for us and that can be scary. We reach a certain age when the body's systems are more likely to shut down than when we were younger. That's unsettling. Think about why a lot of us have life insurance. We don't think about it as much when we're in our 20's, because that's something "old people" have. Well, yeah, but guess what? Now we do too. And part of the necessary maturing we do includes thinking about days when we're not here, and doing our best to leave others who rely on us in as healthy a position as possible.

But if we think about it, life insurance itself is really based on fear. If it's not based on fear itself, it's at least based on the uncertainty surrounding when something will happen, not if. So, there's a mild, subconscious fear we live with every time we pay those life insurance premiums. You can say this about any kind of insurance policy. Responsible people call it "planning", of course!

Fear, however, can be more serious than just this light-hearted example. It can be <u>crippling</u> for us middle-aged people if we don't realize it. We're worried about putting our kids through school, how we're going to retire, what we're going to leave behind, how we're going to care for our family members or friends. To speak nothing of when the heck we're going to live the lives we want and enjoy more of it. It seems to us that most of our time is spent planning for things that we generally have no assurances of happening in a nice, neat timeframe that we control in the end anyway.

Seems a little insane to me.

In essence, we temporarily lose sight of the present. We <u>suffer</u> based on the unknown and what's in the distance. In that way, it emphasizes this: life definitively is not about suffering, but one can see that for some people it is about fear...which then causes suffering. Solve or manage fear, then we solve or at least manage a lot of suffering better.

Some of us will pause here and say, "you can suffer from the past and not just from fear of the future!"

Let's use a real-life example of when a close relative has passed away. We're sad and upset. At its core, our suffering is that that person isn't here anymore. Today. And that they aren't going to be here going forward. Tomorrow. Our fear of going through life without them in the future causes us to suffer more than just remembering their life that's now in the past. That's the root of it. It becomes more about "what are we going to do without them" (going forward) and "I will really miss them not being here" (in the future) than it is about suffering over memories of them even if they happen to be bad ones. It's that we have a hard time reconciling what the future looks like with a big part of our past gone. What we once knew, or what was once so familiar, suddenly becomes a place of uncertainty and discomfort.

So, there's fear and uncertainty in that for most of us that we must now manage. How does one manage fear of tomorrow so that we limit suffering today?

It becomes deeply personal and unique. We can take advice, anyone's advice, and we're still left with choices that are ours and ours alone. This sentence is at the very heart of our responsibilities in middle age. We have experience, we have resources to become more knowledgeable, we may even have a great game plan of how to move forward. We can solicit all the advice in the world. Qualified advice. Good advice. But only we alone can act.

Ultimately, understanding that our choices are our own and taking total and complete responsibility for those choices is a necessary starting point. Gone are the days when we can blame someone, say we didn't know better or pass the buck. This life is our life now. Don't like our boss at work? Big deal. We can choose whether to put up with it or not. What we choose always has consequences – maybe a lighter paycheck, or a change in lifestyle in this case – but nonetheless it's a choice we have. In a terrible marriage? There's a choice. It could be a hard one, yes, with a lot of name-calling and blame spread around, but a choice, nonetheless. Still dealing with a toxic parent? That's a choice too. We can walk away knowing the risks of doing that.

Embracing the fact that everything in life right now is a choice that we have total control over helps to manage fear of situations where we have no control. No one at this point is making us do anything. It's just us, our conscience, our belief system, and where we place the most meaning, that we contend with and answer to.

We could feel differently tomorrow, too! What we believe is the right mindset or behavior today to manage fear, might need to be different next month or next year. Our tendency is to hang onto things for decades sometimes purely because it's comfortable and familiar. We're good at talking ourselves into a whole bunch of excuses when there's an uncertain outcome or risk of failure.

Want to learn a new skill? "Too old for that."

No, we're not.

Want to meet someone new and exciting? "Those days have passed us by."

No, they haven't.

Change careers at our age? "It's too late for us."

It's not too late.

Come back from decades of drug abuse and get clean? "We're junkies, losers, and our ship has sailed."

No, we're not. And, no, it hasn't.

In middle age, especially, we default to a place where it becomes more difficult to leave our comfort zones. But when we're <u>forced</u> to leave our comfort zone, we panic and become fearful. So, isn't it better to leave our comfort zone, or get used to leaving our comfort zone, on our terms rather than have it thrust upon us with no choice?

The answer is yes. Lots of us get used to life being a certain way, and anything that disrupts that way of life becomes scary and unfamiliar. Disruption is an ingredient of fear. If we're the ones choosing to disrupt our own status quo, even in small ways, it sure feels a lot better than having the disruption just land on us.

One idea is to start simple and do small things to change up the status quo and move out of our comfort zones even slightly. If we're used to getting out of bed at 6AM every day, what if we <u>choose</u> to get out of bed at 5AM every day? What would we do with the extra hour that we chose to have? Would we exercise? Would we write? Would we meditate? Would we learn something new?

Even a change that small in nature can make a massive difference in our ability to adapt and embrace discomfort on our own terms. It creates a mindset that we're ready and able to handle anything "different" than the status quo. The more we start to make small changes that cause us minor yet manageable disruption on our terms, the more we'll become less fearful of potential major disruptions and uncertainties that don't happen on our terms.

*

Those who are unwilling or unable to travel down unknown roads will always be our loudest critics when we travel ours.

Proceed anyway.

*

Shifting Our Paradigms

Think of a paradigm as a pattern or model to our lives. In essence, a paradigm encompasses our life's choices up to this point. It's our set of thought patterns, or our default mental programming that we use or fall back on in any given situation. When we are faced with a decision, have pressure put on us, or experience something joyous, our mind and thought patterns immediately go <u>here</u>, wherever here is for you.

What attributes our own paradigms have can be any number of things. They can be optimistic, pessimistic, safe, risky, skeptical, open, patient, hurried, anxious, chaotic, calm, methodical, trusting, gullible, or about a hundred other things. But at this point in our lives, we know what we're all about through our own experiences. If we're honest, we know what our thought paradigms probably are.

So, how have our paradigms served us? Are there things we would change about our default mindset and programming in certain situations? It's a good time for us to take stock of that and be mindful about the approach we choose to take in the coming years. Don't like your paradigm? Be honest about it, focus on it and change it. Is one of our paradigms something we've carried for generations that doesn't serve us anymore that we need to get rid of? Now's the time.

The most important part of this exercise is going through this self-evaluation with brutal honesty. There can be paradigms and mindsets we default to that we're proud of. There can be paradigms and mindsets we've denied for years that we haven't wanted to address.

But we also know that the sooner we address these once and for all and be proud of the way all our paradigms are programmed (or re-programmed) within us, the more freedom we will enjoy and the more confidence we'll have that our paradigms will serve us well. Our default settings might need a midlife cleaning, is all.

Mine sure needed some tweaking. For years, I carried with me some pride about how much I could handle – workwise, personally, emotionally – and how I could keep pushing forward no matter what the amount was "unfazed". My default setting was "pile stuff on, I can handle it." In recent years, I have fundamentally changed this particular paradigm: to know what my limits are and be honest with myself about what I will do, what I won't do, and what I will accept for myself and the behaviors happening around me. Once my default settings changed, my behavior followed, too. It sounds simple, but it has been a major shift, a worthy shift. I now know how to be more efficient in my life and have much more stringent boundaries especially as they relate to relationships. But I first had to accept that my paradigm wasn't serving me well anymore and needed changing.

*

It is not the critic who counts; nor the man who points out how the strong man stumbles, or where the doer of deeds could have done them better. The credit belongs to the man who is actually in the arena, whose face is marred by dust and sweat and blood; who strives valiantly; who errs, who comes short again and again, because there is no effort without error and shortcoming; but who does actually strive to do the deeds; who knows the great enthusiasms, the great devotions; who spends himself in a worthy cause; who at the best knows in the end the triumph of high achievement, and who at the worst, if he fails, at least fails while daring greatly, so that his place shall never be with those cold and timid souls who neither know victory nor defeat.

- Theodore Roosevelt

*

Impermanence

If we're pushing 50 years of age or have already crossed that threshold, we hate to think of this truth: the sun is setting more than its rising.

Knowing what we know after our years of living, we have become acutely aware that everything is temporary. We're all just renting space here. When we go, there's little left behind but memories and legacies. Those count for a lot, to be sure, but we're still referred to in the past tense.

Depending on what you believe the afterlife entails, our spirit might live on, but our physical body is not here. All our stuff is just sitting in the same place we left it. The mementos that meant a lot to us are left with far lesser meaning. The money we worked so hard for is left for other people to enjoy. Everything that was once ours has lost its original owner.

Looked at this way, doesn't it make you worry a lot less about the small stuff? Sweating over minutiae and wasting any precious mental energy on things that don't matter isn't worth it.

*

Emotional Versatility

Lots of us preach about, and hold in high regard, competence as one of the overarching virtues in our lives. Competence is a superpower. But there's another aspect that needs to be part of every man's toolkit as they advance through these stages of life: versatility. This means possessing not only the skill but the adaptability to occasionally veer from who we are at our core in order to return to our core even stronger.

If that sounds confusing, here's an example using compassion. If we're compassionate individuals, it could mean we are polite, empathetic, patient, and we enjoy seeing other people generally happy. Considered by many to be noble qualities, for sure.

But at some point, we might come to understand that these qualities can be taken advantage of or manipulated. When this happens, it leaves compassionate souls frustrated. Having the versatility to be compassionate <u>and</u> set proper boundaries, even if it means being firm or harsh occasionally, will ultimately return us stronger and entrench us more firmly to the basic compassionate beings we are rather than fundamentally changing us into bitter people. We learn how to use the word "no", which might seem like we're veering away from compassion. But saying "no" has nothing to do with being compassionate or not. It is often a necessary step to resetting ourselves.

Let's take another example: optimism. If we're basically optimistic people and believe that the universe is generally a positive force, there are still myriad things that can put a dent in our psyche. Surround ourselves with the wrong type of energy-draining people, and soon we might find ourselves adopting their negative points of view. It can almost seeps= into our subconscious! The thing that the eternal optimist wrestles with is not seeing things as they really are but, rather, as what he or she wishes they could be. In our own optimistic way, we convince ourselves that the ugly truth isn't all that ugly. When the reality is that it may very well be.

For optimists in this case, having the versatility to self-reflect once a week or once a month is a good way to allow things that maybe aren't so pleasant to get into our psyches without dwelling on them and changing our fundamental outlook. Call it a once-weekly or once-monthly reality check. If we walked around every day for a year or years believing everything was just peachy and that no unpleasant truths needed our attention, that would be denial. A state of denial is never a place optimists want to spend any time in. They might have these tendencies but adding a little bit of versatility to look at things as they are is an important overall skill towards achieving higher awareness.

Part of the formula for us middle-aged men is to be true to who we are – the best version of ourselves that we can remember – and develop ways to temporarily stray from that as needed and in healthy ways. By doing so, it allows us to recharge our attitudes with greater conviction and dedication.

*

Sometimes, you must toot your own horn.

No one else will toot it for you, and there are lots of people that could decide to piss in it first.

*

Self-Respect

If we hold ourselves to high standards, we immediately start to attract and find "our people". The more value we place on ourselves and celebrate who we are and our very reason for being, the more we will attract like-minded people who likewise feel good about themselves. Be around people who have high degrees of self-respect and by extension it consistently motivates us to become better ourselves.

There are casualties in this process of building high levels of self-respect. The people in our personal or professional lives who don't meet the very expectations we set for ourselves will stick out quite quickly. Sometimes, it takes a span of weeks or months. Sometimes, years. But ultimately, we all reveal ourselves.

Likewise, if we don't have a very strong opinion about ourselves, we'll attract and start to associate with people at that same stage of their journey too. If we consistently surround ourselves with toxic people, we will ultimately become toxic, too, if we stick around long enough.

Most middle-aged men would agree that being idolized or idolizing another person is not something we do, strive for or even contemplate. Respect, however, is something important. Admiration would be great to have – especially from our innermost circle of people who are supposed to love us unconditionally and without judgment – but we'll settle for a healthy dose of respect! Perhaps what we're asking for is people to <u>recognize</u> the ground we walk on, the path we travel, and admire our years of wisdom, learning and in some cases struggling.

But guess what? Whether or not other people respect us or admire us doesn't matter. At all. All that matters is the degree of self-respect we have for ourselves; not what other people decide to give us.

Healthy relationships build us up and develop us. Dysfunctional ones chop us down and stunt our growth. In one, we're allowed - encouraged, even - to become our fullest and most actualized self. In the other, we're discouraged – figuratively cut down at the knees, even – in becoming our best version.

Which do we prefer? Getting to that point of saying "yes, I've earned not only another person's respect but my own first and foremost" is a giant leap towards self-actualization. It's something to have in our midlife toolkits.

No One Cares About Your Problems

Recently, I conducted an informal poll. I purposely conducted it on a day that was a little less chaotic with work and timed during the holiday season when it gives everyone a chance to wish each other well. I wanted to see, out of all the people I directly interacted with during an entire day, how many of them took the time to wish me well, provide holiday greetings, or in any way took an ounce of time to ask about anything outside of what they wanted from me. This poll spanned some family, some friends, a gas station attendant, people I interacted with related to work, retail store clerks, a dry cleaner, a coffee shop barista, and a few strangers. Here are the results:

- Number of unique individuals interacted with in person, over text, over email, or over video conference: 52
- Out of those, the number of people who made any mention of anything outside of what they wanted or needed from me. Things that qualified were "are you excited for your holidays?", or "what's new with you this week?", or "how's your family doing?": 7

- Out of those 7 people, the number who wished me happy holidays <u>after</u> I wished <u>them</u> happy holidays: 5 (not even all 7!)

There you have it, folks. 5 out of 52 I would count as somewhat deeper than surface-level interactions. Less than 10%. Are these results disheartening? Yes. Are they surprising? No. Does everyone just dislike me? I don't know, maybe! Is everyone totally preoccupied in their own stuff? Yes, probably.

Or it could just be that very few people really give a shit about the daily machinations of our lives. In the grand scheme of things, day in and day out, the reality is that few folks outside your closest circle really care either way. It's true what one of my mentors, Lou Holtz, said: "90% of the people don't want to hear about your problems. The other 10% are glad you have them."

*

Manifesting from True Belief

Another mentor of mine, Dr. Wayne Dyer, said once about manifesting outcomes: "manifesting is not about attracting what you want. Manifesting is an awareness and understanding that you attract what you are." You visualize your goal, be clear about what you want, have faith in who and what you are, and then you expect results as if they have already happened.

Some of the deepest mysteries of life are unlocked by pondering things that only we can answer for ourselves. What can we envision for ourselves in our wildest imaginations? How best do we focus our energy to manifest the outcomes we can envision? How do we "walk the walk" in terms of who and what we are?

The answer to all these questions is the word belief. If you can envision it, it can happen. Then, we must focus all our energies on it. Underlying all of this is the unwavering belief it not only will happen but is in the process of happening.

In essence, manifesting your desires from true belief no longer becomes a question of "if"; instead, we turn it into a question of "when". When we know how to ask for it from ourselves and from the universe, it will be ours. In fact, it already is. We must learn how to ask with perfect clarity, specificity and certainty, though, and focus our energies on the belief that whatever it is we have imagined for ourselves has already happened or is on its way.

*

If one advances confidently in the direction of his dreams, and endeavors to live the life which he has <u>imagined</u>, he will meet with a success unexpected in common hours.

- Henry David Thoreau

*

Stuff is Heavy, Sometimes

At some point in every middle-aged man's life, the challenges we face will seem unfair or extraordinary, and the weight of the world will feel heavy. There will be times when we will wonder, is this it? Is this what's in store for us? Is <u>this</u> how we live the rest of our years?

These questions spur more questions than answers. Like, where do men turn when things are heavy? Do we really have nowhere else to go for information or perspectives? Where do we go in order to find answers to <u>our</u> unique challenges and choices?

So many answers are already expected of us. They come in the form of standards already placed upon us by society, family members, our surname, or our title. But what if we don't have answers and find ourselves searching, as is apt to happen from time to time?

Remember that life happens around us. Things happen around us. Relationships happen with us and largely around us. There are a million things happening around us that we cannot control. Even if we think we can control how individual pieces or aspects of our lives play out, we really can't. The good, the bad or the ugly...they all pass eventually, and we truly have very little say-so about it. If we pride ourselves on being a "boss" or even running our own household, we know that in an instant we can be demoted, or it can all change.

The only thing we have control of is how we choose to respond to life as it happens around us. We're less a protagonist than we like to think, and more often a bystander if we're honest. This simple fact relieves a lot of pressure for a lot of people.

But at some point, everything has or is going to go south on us at least one time. Not for everyone but for most of us. It could be physical, emotional, spiritual, financial, or all of them. And we will wonder if this is it, is this how we end?

Hopefully, the answer is that we accept the heaviness, and we dust ourselves off repeatedly. We get good at recognizing what we really can control, and we get to work. We start collecting little wins. We keep our mouths shut. We make incremental progress, however small. We trust that the process is difficult and long, but we still have faith that it is right. We commit or re-commit to our purpose however many times necessary.

If we do this, one day we will look up and realize that everything that went south on us is behind us, in the distance. It passed. We see in front of us a different landscape now, one that in no way resembles the vantage point we came out of that seemed so murky, dense and heavy.

It's then that it hits us: this is _why_ we continue forward, why it is necessary to uncover our true inner belief systems that perhaps have been lying dormant for years or decades. The hard road reveals our immense character and the work we've done and shows us how we have responded by meeting the crucial and most challenging moments.

It's our choice to respond positively to the heaviness of life, going forward no matter what, taking each day as it comes. Regardless of what is happening around us, we know we're capable of intense focus and we realize that the only thing we can control is how we respond to whatever life throws at us.

When we start to come out of a proverbial fog, of course, we'll feel great. That too shall pass! But no matter, we already have a formula for life that will guide us through the tough times if they happen again. And as the years pass, we understand that each moment, and each response we choose to make to those moments, pass by and then repeat. And repeat again. Things are cyclical. And each time, we have one choice and one choice only which is how we want to respond to the demands of whatever is being placed on us.

The choices we make in terms of how we think is the difference between being average and extraordinary. That's all it is. It isn't about our wealth, our status, our looks or who we know. If we choose to respond to what's placed in front of us at any given time with apathy and defeat, we'll struggle to meet average. If we choose to respond with commitment and positivity, we'll have no problems hitting extraordinary. Sometimes in life, we'll jump in and out of both. But often, how we choose to respond to the intense moments – all of which will indeed pass eventually anyway – will correlate to our well-being and success.

*

Things We Were Taught

We were taught or fed certain things when we were younger that need another look. You know some of them. Don't show weakness. If you have a weakness, improve it. Work on your weaknesses to turn them into strengths. Elite or extraordinary people never have weaknesses or problems. Problems are for average people. The more extraordinary you are, the less likely you'll struggle. No one likes a C-student. You must get all A's to get into a good school and have a better future. Failure is never an option. Hard work means nothing if it doesn't produce perfect results. Strive for perfection. The more famous you are, the better you are as a person. Rich people have it easier. Rich people are happier. You will succeed in life if you just work hard.

Each of these things we may have been taught eventually turn out to be inaccurate, short-sighted or categorically false. Please don't work on your weaknesses more than you leverage your strengths! What about working hard and being guaranteed success? Not always true. Most successful people work hard, but you could very well work hard and still fail.

Rich people are happier? Rich people may not struggle in terms of the financial aspects of life, but some of the most miserable people I've known throughout my life are wealthy. Problems are something that only average people have? No, potential problems are for everyone, until we realize that there are no problems for us, only choices.

When we're told certain things as a younger person, we tend to believe them. They stick with us. We take them to heart. To some extent, we start living our lives in accordance with them and form certain paradigms around them that guide us through school and our early career. As adults, we must unlearn a lot of things!

In essence, the things we're taught involve looking outward for things and seeking, searching, driving, aiming, and obtaining. We're taught through years of formal schooling all about the things in life and how to get them. We're taught very little about the traits we need in life. We're taught very little about who the person is inside of us and then how to foster that properly. We're taught far less about the phrases and qualities related to who we are such as looking within, appreciating, staying positive, being open, being kind, trusting, and smiling.

The searching, the seeking, the striving, the work...it's all about finding a purpose. And when we realize that one of our purposes is simply to find what our capacity is as human beings, we can only then begin to understand what it takes to be extraordinarily self-actualized. We can start by knowing that our presence on this earth by itself was an extraordinary act. By extension, each experience and interaction we go through is extraordinary.

We can still have plenty of goals in life, but they're a lot tougher to get to without the qualities of belief, self-respect, boundaries, commitment, and discipline. It's a good time to be focusing inward and abandoning some of the patterns of thinking we may have learned in our youth.

*

Author's Meditation: Forgiveness

I often listen to audio from the aforementioned Dr. Wayne Dyer and have always found striking similarities between a few of his life experiences and mine. I suppose I relate to the content of his stories and his way of storytelling. He was outspoken about one poignant time period in his life, when he visited his father's grave and forgave him. For decades, he carried unspoken rage and anger directed at his father. Maybe with good reason, too, if you heard his whole story. But the moment he stood at his father's grave and forgave him for all the wrongdoings, his own life changed for the better. All the toxicity was released. A weight was lifted. He could move on with his life effortlessly. That day, being at his dad's grave, was a day that for years he lived in fear of. Yet, afterwards, he described his life becoming easier, more joyful, more productive, and lighter.

I have always said that grudges do nothing but stricken the beholder. Wayne's experiences back that up too.

How does this relate to me? Because for years I blamed others on at least a subconscious level for not supporting me, not supporting my relationship with my daughters, trying to take my money, taking steps to harm me and for not getting the karmic punishment I felt was deserved. Lots of us feel this with an Ex, a coworker, or a so-called friend.

While I am so proud on the surface of all the changes I made in my life to be exactly who I am today, there was that deep feeling inside me of resentment that was the last piece to shake off in my journey of self-actualizing. And the time for me to finally and completely let it go has thankfully come and gone. Not without the occasional frustration, but the deeply rooted blame, resentment and grudge is lifted.

What I deemed as destructive actions towards me by others I let creep into then-current day relationships before I was able to forgive. I had forgotten all about a saying that I really like: "heal the wounds someone has left on you or else you'll bleed on people who had nothing to do with how those wounds got there." For a while, I carried concerns with me that I might one day again hear terrible words used against me, be deceived, be kneecapped, or be hurt.

But that attitude is not fair to anyone in the present day, and forgiveness is necessary in order to get out of that emotional place. The actions and trauma caused by one person are unrelated to another person. Besides, it's my issue. It's my thing to deal with or at least not let bother my life in the present or any opportunities my life has presented me with since then.

So, the heaviest of the weights of having to forgive were lifted. I might get annoyed from time to time, but I no longer carry around this fear that the same thing will happen to me again. Fear that my new life will start to resemble my old one. Fear that signs I see daily are the universe playing dirty tricks on me again. Fear that my suspicion of people's motives isn't as pure as mine.

So, I decided no more living in fear. Yes, everything in my new life could happen exactly how it did in my old one. I believe it won't. But it could. The difference now is that there's no fear and no resentment of what used to drag me down. Only forgiveness and looking ahead. I'll deal with whatever happens in the future when or if it meets me in the present day.

Now, years later, with a great wife, new baby boy, new career, new house, and some new friends (along with some of the great old friends), my life in no way resembles the one from before. Even if it all went to hell in a handbasket again, it wouldn't be the same. There are zero grudges. Zero fears. My health is fantastic. It's been a remarkable transformation, and I too often don't appreciate it or the work I have done to get here.

But the last piece of the puzzle is usually the hardest. I think I have found it much the same way Wayne Dyer did when he released himself from the target of his frustration - his father - and got rid of the power that was holding him hostage all those years. He found it in forgiveness.

And now, like Wayne, I have metaphorically largely let go of my past traumas. Letting go of the negative emotions associated with a horrible time period. Releasing the targets of my deepest anxieties. For now, I will continue to try and be there for all my kids as best I can to support them and count all my blessings for this life.

So, yes, the universe has gotten a lot out of me and my life. I have more to give, and the only thing that had been holding me back from soaring to greater heights again was me. It's because I hadn't fully released my grievances stemming from my own belief system that if people do things destructively and dangerously, there should be some penalty. Some comeuppances.

Guess what? You could wait forever, and it might never happen. Who cares? I was the only one that was holding out for that, rather than just forgiving people and moving on. The last thing I believe is that there are comeuppances. Everything evens out, I just may not know about it. And that's okay.

By releasing emotions that weren't allowing me to truly forgive, it's my time, and my family's and friend's time, to be grateful and forward-looking in life instead of backpedaling. If a different fate awaits me or knocks me from my path again, I'll deal with it if the time comes.

*

I forgive you. You are released.

And therefore, I am released.

*

No Justified Resentments

There is no such thing as a justified resentment.

If we still carry resentments with us, make it priority number one to do away with them. Carry no baggage in the form of resentments towards anyone no matter how wrongly anyone treated us. Getting ridding of resentments will set us free once and for all.

Further, no longer should we surround ourselves with people who carry resentments with them, especially if they try and convince us they're justified. The longer we hang around those people, the more <u>we</u> become the target of all their resentments. And these resentments will have nothing to do with us. Don't walk away from these people. Run.

*

"Do not allow my confidence to offend your insecurities."

- Deion Sanders

*

Our Imagination is <u>Still</u> Important

Too few of us realize that the things we haven't yet experienced are still possible even as we get older. We lose our imagination. We stop dreaming. We stop envisioning outcomes.

Our imagination cannot be contaminated with thoughts of what used to be. It also can't be clouded in negativity. We don't allow others to pollute or set our limitations for us. We don't allow others to judge or dictate what our personal capabilities are or can be. No one else can define our human capacity. When others speak to us in this regard, they speak not of what <u>we're</u> capable of, but of the limitations in which <u>they</u> are most saddled by.

The truly self-actualized (and even divine) know the following about limitations and capacity: that each soul is limitless. Whatever we can imagine for ourselves, we can be or achieve. Still. If we can dream it, it can happen. This rule always applies no matter how old we are or what stage of life we're in.

*

Misery

Stop arguing in favor of your misery. If you keep making arguments for your misery, you're guaranteed to win them all.

*

A millionaire won't judge you for wanting to start a business.

A bodybuilder won't judge you for wanting to work out and get in shape.

A professional basketball player won't judge you for wanting to play a pickup game.

It's always the people going nowhere who judge you for taking the necessary steps to do something new and good with your life.

*

"I trained four years to run 9 seconds."

- Usain Bolt

…And yet, there are people who give up when they don't see results in a week or a month.

*

Author's Meditation: Your Story is <u>Yours</u>

We have the choice, the right and even the responsibility to the following: we take control of our stories, our narratives and don't let other people talk about our life or our life stories. They're ours, and ours alone to talk about. We mustn't listen to someone else's version or interpretation of what we have experienced, no matter who they are. We've earned this right and obligation to ourselves, middle-aged men.

Gone, now, is anything from your past you aren't proud of. Gone, now, is everything from the past that you didn't get the chance to tell <u>your</u> way exactly how <u>you</u> experienced it.

Instead, here, today for all of us, is truth. Here, today, is you telling it like it is even if it upsets someone. Your truth is often difficult to take because it's not convenient for other people. Your truth, especially if it's been kept under wraps for years, might be particularly difficult for others to even bear.

Tell it anyway.

The next generation needs to hear your truth from you, not someone else. It's your responsibility and part of your legacy to do it especially if you've encountered some real challenges.

Let me give you an example. A personal one.

At age 43, my life unraveled in a big way quickly. For a span of about four or five years afterward, everyone in my family, my ex-family, some of my friends, and even some newer acquaintances had their version of what happened to me. Each version that other people liked to tell seemed to fit their narratives conveniently, yet they never matched my truth or the truth. Even some family or friends who were around me during that time period never wanted to listen to my whole narrative. They would get angry with me when I would be silent or not want to cave into pressure to talk, or for not agreeing with them about the root of my challenges.

The truth is that I had a team of doctors across all disciplines. I had psychologists, physicians, addiction counselors, LCSW's, and brain specialists examine me. Easily over 50 professionals in total in a span of about 18 months. I got to know quite a few of them rather well, too, and so I have a crystal-clear reality of my story. All of it.

The hardest part for me started in May 2017. That month, I was involved in a harrowing automobile accident. My car, with only me in it at the time thankfully, was at a train crossing in Barrington, Illinois. I happened to be square in the path of an 18-wheeler that hadn't cleared a set of train tracks entirely and an active (and speedy) Canadian National freight train. They collided into one another and then into me. The accident was not my fault. I was simply in the wrong place at the wrong time. I came out of the wreck largely unscathed physically. Except...

I hit my head very badly at impact and suffered a severe concussion. This was on the heels of having had two of them previously in my life. To say that this experience stayed with me for some time is an understatement. By the third one, it's not something you can easily just shake off.

Still, the following week after that I was to start a new management job. I did, but my brain was not right. I told Human Resources at the company on my first day of work what had happened. They were horrified. I had severe headaches daily, and never said anything else to anybody. There was no one really to tell anyway. For the first time ever, I had what doctors later told me were panic attacks. I tried to exercise but would occasionally just pass out. Just out of the blue. That happened three times. I was a former professional athlete, and so I knew my body. I knew all kinds of things were wrong but didn't know what.

I was also going through a divorce. There was stress.

By late June, a month or so after the impact of the crash, I was learning about all different pain medications and how they might become available to me. Quite easily, I must say. To say I was a master mixologist with pills would probably be kind. Most of the time, it was over-the-counter overdosing. Sometimes, the harder stuff. I knew a guy. You know what also went great with them at the time I thought? Vodka. Or at least it was the only thing that worked to numb things to a manageable level.

I progressively got worse, fast. And my head didn't get any better. I remember feeling my brain moving around in my head on some days. I remember sitting at home on weekend days in the dark. The light of day was too bright sometimes. I remember not being able to handle any load on my brain, whether it was work, paperwork, personal stuff, or even just planning a time to meet a friend. I remember asking God to somehow find me a way to get better. I was incapable of making any type of decision, which I later found out (from a doctor, not an armchair quarterback) was because of the damage to my brain initially stemming from the concussions.

The very next month, I was at a professional baseball stadium in Chicago as part of a corporate event. It was a splendid night and since it was a corporate event, we had the whole stadium to ourselves. Batting practice, shagging fly balls, running around on the field, food, drink, the whole thing. At the end of this very fine event, I hopped on a red line train to go home. I called a friend, Lynda. She is the only person in the world who knows the details of this particular story and could tell it with the exact specificity I can.

While I was on the phone with her, the train pulled into a station. The Jackson Street stop, which was underground. The train doors opened, and shots rang out. Lynda's voice was screaming through the phone, "Mike, were those gun shots?"

End call.

Immediately after I heard bullets, I watched one pierce through the window over my right shoulder and saw one of the gunmen hop up from his squatted position next to the train door to whip out a gun and return fire. I was in the middle of a gunfight alright.

Like everyone else on the train, I hit the floor. Everyone searched for a way to get underneath seats. I found cover, but on the way down, hit my head hard. Again. Another concussion. I remember looking out from underneath the seat, into the aisle, and seeing black boots slowly pacing. A teenage girl was sobbing from underneath a seat across the aisle. She mouthed at me "I don't want to die." I remember mouthing back "it's going to be okay."

After about a minute of silence, I was the first one on the train to poke my head up. I motioned to the girl from across the aisle to come with me. We crawled to the train door, I looked out onto the platform, heard a few more gun shots from farther down the platform, and figured we had a window to run.

She grabbed my hand, and we ran up the stairs to the street. At the top of the stairs, our hands dislodged. She went one way, and I went the other. I never saw her again.

Of course, that latest brush with catastrophe did nothing for my mental health or my physical health. My head hurt so badly I thought it might explode. I devolved. I felt alone. Today, I almost can't believe I was the main character in these stories that happened so closely together. At the time, I felt like no one back home would understand. Bad changes were happening in my head, my habits, and I knew they were happening. I figured out a way to control the pills, but not the drinking. I couldn't stop. It was like my mind was well enough to know I was making my brain worse, but it wasn't well enough to make me stop. I was at the mercy of gripping addictions without the ability to function properly. I was in a lot of physical pain. I was headed down, way down, quickly.

It got worse and worse for several months, until I was back in my hometown for Christmas. On Christmas morning, after a day and night of heavy self-medicating, I landed in an ER with a 251/140 blood pressure, and with death closing in on me fast. Just ask the hospital priest at my bedside while I was shackled to it. For an entire week, I was in a bed. I wasn't dead, but I was in a vegetable state.

With the help of my family - my core family of my parents, my sister and her family - I was sent to a facility for rehabilitation. No one else did anything. I suppose there were at least a few people who tried to pour more gasoline on the dumpster fire that was me, but that was about it.

At this facility, I was in rough shape and couldn't be admitted initially. I was far too weak. I couldn't walk, talk, write or eat by myself. Eventually, it was there, after several weeks, that I could walk again without the aid of a wheelchair or a walker. I relearned how to walk. Soon after, I relearned how to communicate. Then, the fine motor skills started to come back. Eventually, I learned a lot about what I had been through and specifically what I put myself (and others) through. I learned all about my brain and TBI. I learned all about addiction. I learned all about psychological conditions like narcissistic personality disorder, and what happens to people like me who had been exposed to it. I worked my ass off to get better. Once hopeless, I eventually regained my hope and then my strength. I spent three full months at the facility and did everything and more that I was asked to do. I started leading groups and talking to other people who needed help. I made quite a few new friends at the time, too.

And I'll never forget the letters I received from friends during those three months.

The climb back for me was slow, but necessarily so. Other people to this day very badly want to talk about my accidents. Or my addiction, and my accelerated seven months or so of heavy dosing and drinking. They really want just <u>one</u> thing or <u>one</u> <u>problem</u> to point to as the narrative of my story even to this day. I can only say: take your pick from about 20 things!

People who want to tell your story, or parts of it, with their narrative are being selfish. I've learned that when other people try and tell your story, there's a bent to it. A bias. There are important things that get glossed over or forgotten. As important as the education that I had to learn for myself was, it was equally important for me to know and understand <u>everything</u> I was going through in its entirety and its complexity. It was an interconnected web of functions that were simultaneously failing. The accidents, the concussions, the marital situation, the self-medicating. If you believe in luck, there was probably some bad luck sprinkled in there too.

Left to other people's devices, though, I could be called a bad husband, a junkie, a bad employee, a bad dad, or a sick mental patient with a very damaged brain. Maybe I was one or all those things, to some people, at one point in time. I don't know. But maybe I'm whichever one is most convenient for other people to use to tell the story that they want to tell.

And that to me is wrong.

The good news is that I don't think I'm any of those things at all. And that's the point. It's not someone else's life story. My life is not beholden to someone else's interpretation of it. The same thing goes for you and your story. My story is based on facts, and a very specific set of circumstances that can be a cautionary tale for those who follow. It's my right, responsibility and even obligation to others to tell it if it can help someone get through a rough patch. Maybe it helps someone or gives one person hope. That would be great.

Don't be dragged backwards. The purpose of recovering from awful things is so that you don't have to live inside those awful things ever again, and so you can speak your truth about them on your terms, in your timeframe, and in your context. No one has your perspective or your truth. Only you do. So, speak your truth. Tell your story – the good, bad and ugly - when, where and with whomever you want.

*

"There is nothing noble in being superior to some other man. True nobility is in being superior to your former self."

-    Ernest Hemingway

PART II: The Covenants

I, Middle-Aged Man:

The Covenants

The following covenants can be helpful, quick reminders used occasionally. Or, when we choose, they are commitments we can make for a healthier, more purposeful, more effective, self-actualized life.

Starting Out Each Day

I, middle-aged man, for as long as I am physically able, vow to get out of bed and face the day with as much rigor and optimism as I can muster. Even if I have unexplainable back aches, random leg cramps or other ailments to contend with, I make no excuses for my condition. No matter what other external factors are present in my life that I'm facing each day, I make no excuses for my mood.

Discipline to Achieve Freedom

I, middle-aged man, believe that from discipline comes personal freedom, not the other way around. I know that to achieve financial freedom it requires discipline in managing my money. I know that to achieve organizational freedom, I must be disciplined in showing up for work and contributing. I know that to achieve spiritual freedom, I must be disciplined in my self-care practices and how I train my mind. I do not get distracted by people who mistake freedom for chaos.

Managing Emotions

I, middle-aged man, commit to managing my emotions when unexpected news comes my way. I understand that I possess the power to choose my emotional response to events out of my control no matter how difficult it may be. I accept the fact that grief, shock, sadness or confusion will be present for all people, including me. But, by virtue of my age and life experience, I recognize my responsibility to be a pillar of strength for myself and others. I accept shock, grief, sadness, unease and uncertainty. My ability to maintain balanced emotions, appreciation and perspective after those initial emotions subside allow me to continue moving forward respectfully and peacefully.

Sometimes, Shut Up and Go to Bed

I, middle-aged man, know that sometimes it's okay to simply shut my mouth and go to bed. After a hard day, the right thing to do may be to accept it all and put my head on the pillow at 8pm. I don't let one rough day turn into a rough week, month or year.

Embrace a Higher Calling

I, middle-aged man, know that having the opportunity to mentor someone is one of the highest callings one could be fortunate enough to have. It reenforces that I'm doing something right in my life. Having the opportunity to share any small bits of wisdom with another person can be invaluable when and if the recipient is willing to hear it. Being in a mentoring frame of mind allows me to continually pay my gratitude forward and show someone else I care.

Let Irritations Go

I, middle-aged man, know that most feelings of frustration I experience are as minor or major as I choose to make them. The more I assign negative energy to difficult moments I encounter, the more likely it is that minor irritations become major roadblocks for me. I let my frustrations pass when they are merely annoyances not when it's too late and they become headaches.

Accept the Past to Stay in the Present

I, middle-aged man, recognize that there are lots of spiritual gurus asking me to subscribe to the notion of always staying present, and "in the moment". What that usually means is not having my mind stray from what is right in front of me. Occasionally, it is nice to take a trip down memory lane for a few minutes, though. I understand it's counterproductive to become stuck or fixated for a long time about my past. My work is here and now.

Leave a Mark, Selectively

I, middle-aged man, allow things to be what they are, good or bad, in the moment. I fight whatever urges I have to leave my stamp, imprint or remark on every little thing. I recognize that most things in life do in fact continue without my touch or say-so. I focus on a few things I'm truly competent in or an expert about and pick my spots about when to leave a more impactful imprint on something.

Embrace Aspects of Spirituality

I, middle-aged man, accept aspects of spirituality because I feel a higher presence in my life. The virtues I embrace include awareness, clarity, and enlightenment. Awareness is what is going on or happening outside of me and inside of me. Clarity is my ability to look at something with a discerning eye and not have any disillusionment about what reality is. Enlightenment is being able to really see how or what things are likely to happen based on the energies around me. It's having in-the-moment precision and a sixth sense of what's to come. I understand these virtues are learned oftentimes over the course of years, and I commit to that.

Accept People's Challenges and Be Gentle

I, middle-aged man, recognize that everyone is struggling with something internally. Every single person is fighting their own battle that I know nothing about. For this reason, I try whenever possible to be gentle in my dealings with people and mindful of the context of each interaction.

"Why Me?"

Why Not Me?

I, middle-aged man, know that in the past I might have asked "why me?" about every single, tiny (in the grand scheme of things), unfortunate thing that happened to me. I had the urge to play the poor victim sometimes. I now realize that if I subscribe to that way of thinking, I'd also have to ask, "why me?" about my blessings. Therefore, the question should be flipped to "why not me", and the answer is because I can handle the challenges and embrace the prosperity that is directed towards me.

What Heroism Really Is

"True heroism is remarkably sober, very undramatic. It is not the urge to surpass all others at whatever cost, but the urge to serve others at whatever cost."

- Arthur Ashe

Being Better Than We Were

I, middle-aged man, continue to experience the cyclical nature of life and know it's more beneficial not to try and be better than others, but to be better than I used to be. I don't forget where I am right now and how far I've come on my own journey. The only thing more that I owe is to myself, not anyone else, and if I focus on being better than I was yesterday then the rest will take care of itself.

People Who Do You Wrong

I, middle-aged man, move above and beyond the people who do me wrong. I know that one of the only things that could hold me back in my journey is a person or maybe a few people that we don't forgive or move on from. No matter what...I forgive someone or something regardless of how much they have wronged me. If someone or something wrongs me again, I will forgive them again. It's my responsibility to move on and flourish, and seeking revenge or getting the last word only prohibits that from happening. I know that grudges do nothing but stricken the beholder.

Appreciate Yourself

I, middle-aged man, will take time to appreciate myself today. To truly bask in the wonder of the human being I am, and how I've evolved. To not only thank those around me but thank myself. I don't utter these sentiments aloud because they're just for me. It's better and a lot less vain to carry my appreciation inside. Besides, very few would understand.

Your Real Inner Circle

I, middle-aged man, understand that my "inner circle" and group of confidantes must be small. 10/80/10. 10% of people I count on as friends <u>are</u> truly my friends, through thick and thin. 80% of people I generally believe are friends are "kind of" my friends...they generally wish me well and under certain circumstances, they'll be there for me. 10% of people I think are my friends are not my friends at all and might be sabotaging me right this minute. Who knows. I hold dear to the first 10%. I'm open, kind and helpful to the 80%. I disengage with, and avoid at all costs, the latter 10% even if it costs me something.

Reflect and Grieve Without Shame

I, middle-aged man, reflect and grieve in my own way with due deference to those loved ones lost, without shame. I take my time and give myself space. I don't make any sudden movements or changes in my life immediately. I give it a minute. I stay in my lane. I'm humbled by death and humbled by continuing life.

Notice Other People's Efforts

I, middle-aged man, notice when others around me step up to help. I appreciate their efforts. I make every effort possible to give gratitude and thanks to them when they do big things and all the little things that help to create positive energy.

Renting v. Owning

I, middle-aged man, realize I am just renting. Renting time. Renting space. Renting precious moments.

The things I too often in the past have held as valuable – things I "own", stuff, possessions, money - are temporary. I can't take anything with me when I depart. Memories are what I hold onto the longest while I am here, not stuff. I try and live well, love well, and take care of those who treat me well while I'm renting.

Gratitude at Work

I, middle-aged man, understand how important it is to carry gratitude with me professionally with people at work. It doesn't matter if I'm in my dream job, or if I'm generally bummed out with my vocation. Inevitably there is someone or perhaps a group of people who shine brightly. I take time to appreciate them.

Alone Time

I, middle-aged man, commit to taking some alone time as often as required in small increments. I look for at least 15-minute breaks during the day. Sometimes, I try for an hour. It might be a brisk run, stretching or some meditation throughout the day. I do my work, do my best, help others when possible, and draw firm boundaries around the time I need to take care of me. I don't apologize for it.

"No"

I, middle-aged man, vow to remember how to say the word "no" and use it, when necessary, kindly and firmly.

Energies

I, middle-aged man, continue to learn that energy works in circular fashion. When I'm with someone, I'm not only opening them up to my energetic state, but I'm absorbing theirs. If I bring a low-vibrational, low-energy state to a specific interaction, I'm saddling another person with the obligation of having to absorb that. If someone else brings a low-vibrational, low-energy state to an interaction with me, I am aware of that, too, in order to not absorb all of it subconsciously. I take necessary steps to protect my energy.

Disappointing Others

I, middle-aged man, realize that disappointing others is a fact of life sometimes even if it's unintentional. I know that disappointing others is far less of a sin than disappointing myself.

Not Getting Too Hung Up on Little Things

I, middle-aged man, will not sweat the small stuff too much. When I notice my anxiety levels being too high about the littlest of things, I agree to stop – full stop – and ask myself, "does this really matter?" In the day-to-day, some small things do matter especially if they impact other people's day-to-day lives. But for most of the mundane little things that don't matter, I recognize when I'm sweating things I shouldn't.

Understanding Basic Needs

I, middle-aged man, know that every human being needs three basic things: 1) to love someone else; 2) for someone else to love us; and 3) to be doing something meaningful with purpose.

Birthdays

I, middle-aged man, vow to always appreciate my birthdays and honor them in my own little way regardless of whether there's a bigger celebration or not. For as long as possible, I focus on my birthday as less of a retrospective and more of a prospective. It's less about looking back for too long, and more about looking ahead and imagining what else this lifetime holds for me going forward.

Keep Going No Matter What

I, middle-aged man, commit to keep on keeping on until my last breath, no matter what tries to knock me down or knock me sideways. I know that sometimes I must grit my teeth and keep going when times are difficult. I know sometimes it just doesn't "feel like my day", and things seem to happen all on top of another. I spill my coffee. My car won't start. I'm late to a meeting, and then another. My child doesn't feel well. All this could happen, and it might only be Noon! If a day isn't going my way and I feel like I'm fighting everything, then I preserve my energy. I simply make it through the day as best I can.

You Become What You Think About

I, middle-aged man, know that if my thoughts focus on negative things, even if they are negative things I am trying to avoid, I will gravitate to them. I will always naturally gravitate towards anything I focus on, even if I'm trying to steer clear of it. That's why it's so important for me to fill my mind with high vibrational energy, positive thoughts, emotions and outcomes. I will only consider best-case scenarios, never worst-case scenarios. The lesson I learn is to focus on where I want to go, not on where I don't want to go.

More Gratitude

I, middle-aged man, make it a point to remind myself often to give gratitude whenever possible. I work on adjusting my "default settings" to seeing the inherent good in everything that occurs around me. It's up to me to interpret (not control) what's happening around me and respond in the healthiest way possible. Which, usually, is to give large amounts of gratitude for everything that I have in my life rather than despair over things I don't.

Appreciate Grace in Others

I, middle-aged man, take the time to learn people's stories, especially people who exhibit the class and grace that I admire in others. When there's a lesson that I can learn from others, I try.

Competitiveness Never Grows Old

I, middle-aged man, welcome competitiveness. It's something I know a lot about, but it's different now. I focus on being competitive with myself and compare myself against my own standards, purpose and potential and not someone else's.

Revel in the Innocence of Youth (Be Silly)

I, middle-aged man, remind myself that I'm never too old to be silly or appreciate other people's silliness. Much like a child or young man isn't jaded or weighed down by expectations, what's "proper", or past experiences, so must I release all of that. As an adult, I may have things built up over time which weighs down my ability to give and receive joyful emotions. It's an important life hack: find joy and lightness in the simple things again. And be silly once in a while.

I'm Enough

I, middle-aged man, am enough.

(And probably more than enough for some.)

Handling Compliments

I, middle-aged man, know that compliments may be given to us on occasion. In the past, I might have been embarrassed by them or brushed them off. I know that they get harder to come by as life progresses, so I embrace and appreciate every compliment or nicety directed at me. I say, "thank you".

Losing Your Job

I, middle-aged man, believe that when my professional fortunes turn, there's likely a much deeper reason that leads to tremendous opportunity for me. If my change in fortunes don't stem from a lack of effort or a true disciplinary reason, I know there's an underlying and much bigger purpose in store. It means I'm not in the right place, maybe never was, and the forces of the Universe are launching me into something else. Sometimes, that's what it takes to change courses, and I feel blessed that I'm free to make the necessary next step in my journey on my own terms.

Confidence

I, middle-aged man, know that confidence without clarity equals chaos. Clarity is a necessary ingredient of confidence, not the other way around. Being able to clearly know what's happening inside of me and clearly see things around me inspires me to take the necessary paths forward in my life confidently.

Blame No One

I, middle-aged man, blame no one else for anything or any circumstance in my life. Ever. As I know, there are no such things as justified resentments, and there's no point in placing blame at anyone else's feet no matter how badly or how wrongly they may have treated me. The second I release all blame from everyone and everything in my life, the lighter and clearer I will become about my present condition and the necessary steps forward. Blame and resentment hold me captive.

Don't Quit

"Don't quit when the tide is lowest, for it's just about to turn;

Don't quit over doubts and questions, for there's something you may learn;

Don't quit when the night is the darkest, for it's just a while 'til dawn;

Don't quit when you've run the farthest, for the race is almost won;

Don't quit when the hill is steepest, for your goal is almost nigh;

Don't quit, for you're not a failure...Until you fail to try."

- Anonymous

Bask in Stillness

I, middle-aged man, believe reading the works of
ancient philosophers is food for the soul. Seneca once
said, "Stillness is The Way". I embrace stillness. I get
excited about simply being still. The biggest
breakthroughs for me professionally, spiritually and
personally have occurred and occur presently during
stillness, never amidst chaos or multi-tasking.

When You're Totally Drained

I, middle-aged man, know it's okay and perfectly natural on some days to feel totally and completely drained, and that it could very well be a sign from the Universe. There are days when it takes every ounce of physical, emotional or spiritual energy to perform the most basic thoughts or behaviors. I know on these days is when I can make the most progress. I know on these days when I have nothing left to give is when I must give more. I know on these days is when I can transcend my own personal expectations. I know on these days that whatever I can do will be considered a triumph and I will celebrate it as such.

Be Astonished by Children

I, middle-aged man, recognize that children possess something valuable: enthusiasm and wonder. Most kids are happy and amazed at seemingly simple or even mundane things. Make no mistake that they have it right; because most things are amazing if I really stop and think about them. The simple act of creating a beautiful bracelet, or reading a certain book, or being overjoyed about a new pair of mittens are all things to be celebrated. Therefore, I'm committed to regaining my boyish enthusiasm for things happening around me with the same fervor as my kids have.

Aging

I, middle-aged man, welcome my own aging process with each passing year. I cherish all the experiences that make up the years I've lived. I cherish that it's been a thrilling, wild ride. Even during the down periods in my life, it's been a thrill to see how each turn turned out. I embrace that I have the emotional battle scars and physical signs of aging that tell my story. I continue to try and manifest outcomes by (re)starting fresh with each passing year.

Old Friends Can Become New Again

I, middle-aged man, take the necessary time to foster old and special friendships. My oldest living friendship began I was 5 years old. I understand that these special friends are part of my inner circle. I am free with them to talk about my hopes for the future and what I hope to manifest. I recognize there's something timeless about old and yet still-close friendships. I appreciate them always.

Asking for Help

I, middle-aged man, know that I'm often not great at asking for help. I vow to know when it's time to put my ego aside and get the necessary assistance if I'm without solutions. It may be a pride thing, an ego thing, or both; for many years, whatever it was that needed figuring out, I always believed that I had the tools and intelligence to figure it out. It has taken me a long time, but I'm understanding that it's impossible to be an expert problem-solver at everything and there isn't a limitless amount of time in a day to do the work either. So, the easier, faster, more efficient and more fun path is to ask for help.

The Merchant and his Parrot

By: Rumi

A Persian merchant got a parrot as a gift from his Indian trading partners and kept her in a cage. The parrot could sing well and every day after work the merchant would enjoy listening to her songs.

When the merchant left for India again, he asked the parrot what she wanted from her country. "I do not need anything, Master," said the parrot, "however, if you see parrots of my family there, tell them that I am trapped in a cage here and that I miss them very much. Ask them whether it was fair that they were free to fly anywhere, while I was slowly dying here in captivity. Ask them also what I should do."

The merchant went to India and one day he did see a group of parrots very much like the one he had in his home. They were happily flying amongst the trees. When the merchant conveyed his parrot's message, one of the parrots fell from the tree and appeared dead. The merchant was distraught at the effect of his message.

He wondered whether that parrot was a relative of his parrot and died from grief.

When the merchant returned home, his parrot asked him whether he had met any parrots of her family. The merchant hesitantly told the parrot what happened. He added, "I'll never forgive myself for causing the poor bird's death. But what's the use? Once the arrow has left the bow it will never return, and so are words that leave our lips."

Before he could finish his sentence, his parrot fell from her perch on to the cage floor, apparently dead. The merchant began to cry, blaming himself for causing another parrot to die. After a while, he opened the cage door, picked up the parrot gently and took her outside. He let her down on the grass and was looking for a place to dig a grave for her.

Suddenly, the parrot flew away and, from the high branch of a tree, told him: "The parrot you saw in India was perhaps not related to me, but her action showed me how I could go free! She helped me understand that my imprisonment was due to my beautiful song, my talent for entertaining you and your guests. My precious voice was in fact the cause of my servitude. By her action, she taught me that my freedom would lie in the act of dying in the sense of forsaking my attachment to my worldly talents, which I had prized so highly." Saying so, the parrot flew away to freedom.

I, middle-aged man, don't let anyone else decide what freedom means to me. I recognize that sometimes it's imperative to let go of things we feel caged by in order to achieve our higher purpose through the freedom necessary to achieve that. And sometimes, it means doing whatever it takes to achieve that freedom.

Motivation

I, middle-aged man, know that our motivation each day is the person staring back at us in the mirror. What can I achieve? How well can I treat people? How can I help other people achieve more? What kinds of things can I do today to make myself better? After the age of 40, using anyone else as motivation is an exercise in futility, frustration, and stupidity.

Choose Fluidity over Rigidity

I, middle-aged man, know the difference between living life rigidly and fluidly. I understand that the main reason why people disagree is due to rigidity. Rigidity in points of view, rigidity in understanding another person's feelings, and rigidity in one's perspective. I know that rigidity is not the same thing as being disciplined or having an established routine. Routines can be great. All high performers follow a disciplined routine when it comes to physical, mental and spiritual well-being. When discipline turns into excess rigidity is when things run awry. This happens when I believe my routine and my discipline can or should work for everyone else in the exact way it does for me.

Life is Not Fair

I, middle-aged man, am certain that life owes me nothing nor is life always fair on any given day. Sometimes society penalizes those who are transparent and honest. Sometimes criminals skate by. Sometimes people treat other people heinously and without civility. Sometimes people you know are con artist with no remorse. Sometimes we suffer consequences of doing good, while others who do "less good" (in our minds) suffer no consequences.

As my long-time tennis coach Bobby Bayliss used to say about life's fairness: "life's a bitch, and then you die." Get over it. I'm not the judge and jury of what's fair, and my moral high ground may not be shared by everyone else.

Stepping Out of Our Comfort Zone

I, middle-aged man, commit to doing something totally out of my comfort zone at least once a month. I'm not a big fan of Fairs, typically. I went to two in a span of a month one year. It's not my thing. It's my wife's thing. Not my thing. Never has been, never will be. To me, they're like cruises. Not a fan because I feel like a floating prisoner. However, I know that each time I take myself out of my comfort zone, I'm growing. It's a continual process of trial, experimentation and refinement necessary to identify my ever-changing limits. I choose to do new things for that very reason.

Where Happiness Comes From

I, middle-aged man, commit to reminding myself that
happiness comes not by what we have, but what we are. What
we are is made up of our character and attitude. It's how we
handle wins and losses; deal with desires attained and desires
denied; alter our perspectives that stem from both achievements
and failures. Our foremost job in this physical world is to
celebrate all of <u>who</u> we are and what we experience. It is not to
count the things we have.

Recognize Your "Why"

I, middle-aged man, take steps to understand my "why" in anything I do. At my core, I create and invent. I love the process of it. No great author or creator is driven by "what's in it for them" as their why. My "why" in anything is always found in two P's: process and principle.

State Your Intentions Clearly

I, middle-aged man, consistently monitor my intentions each day. I used to think intentions were like a running to-do list. I used to be big on listing like 20 goals at the beginning of each year, with my intention of achieving all 20 goals. If I did, it was a good year. If I didn't, I had work to do the following year. Over the years, it started to feel robotic and not fun. After entering a period of greater enlightenment, I've changed my tune. My intentions are not things or acts or lists. I intend to take care of my children until I leave this physical earth. I intend to be a great, thoughtful and fun partner and friend. I intend to, professionally, utilize my life experiences to make a positive impact on others. I intend to vanquish any negative energy or energy-dampening forces in my life. And I intend to be as joyful at my core along the way as possible.

Simplicity is Important and Underrated

I, middle-aged man, seek and appreciate simplicity in my life. I'm mature enough to know that this doesn't mean I aim to skate through life with no challenges or difficulties. I recognize the importance those play in my growth, too. But simplifying life, or at least my outlook on life, is important. Why? Because I know how I feel when something is simple. I feel free. I feel loose. I feel confident. So, I keep my mind open, free and simple so that it can be sharp, fast, and unimpeded.

Other People's Opinions (if they don't impact us)

I, middle-aged man, let go of any angst or frustration at other people's decisions or opinions when they don't impact me. I simply let them go. To each their own. I do not try and convince anyone else to see things my way.

Being Wrong and Making Mistakes is Necessary

I, middle-aged man, celebrate my mistakes and wrong decisions in the past. I've gotten so many things wrong in my life! Lots of do-overs. Lots of restarts. One major life "Rebuild". It's part of the overall journey, which is never supposed to be a straight line from Point A to Point B for anyone. The horizontal axis on a graph of most people's life has got a lot of zigzags. Sometimes, it resembles more of a dot matrix with prominent points that are spread out in randomized fashion over time. But these zigzags or seemingly random dots are not random at all. Our mistakes usually don't stay mistakes for long before they become course-corrections. And each course-correction signifies growth and a new trail yet to be blazed.

Recognize the Passage of Time

I, middle-aged man, commit to never forgetting that times change, and that my life spans multiple generations now. Raising kids today with my son is different from when my two girls were born. I remind myself that each young person's journey today is much different, and in a lot of ways tougher, than mine was decades ago.

Understand Your Resilience

I, middle-aged man, am resilient. I take great pride in surrounding myself with other resilient people, too. Resilience more than any other quality binds like-minded people together.

Create

I, middle-aged man, am a creator and builder. In this context, it means that I no longer look to deconstruct things, take things apart or find fault in things. Instead, I'm in a constant state of creation and building, whether it's personally or professionally. I try to construct and reconstruct rather than tear down.

Failure is Crucial

I, middle-aged man, vow to accept and even embrace failures along the way that teach me valuable lessons. Thousands of stories exist about people we've never heard of who get the motivation to do something hard, often right after a heartbreaking setback. It's easy to work when we're on top and winning in life. It's hard to work when we've suffered defeat or some other negative outcome. The best always find a way, though.

Anger is the Enemy

I, middle-aged man, am consistently baffled by anger and aim
to avoid that emotion at any cost. I avoid other angry people.
Anger always makes headlines, though. Why? Because it's
often shocking and almost always <u>disruptive</u>. At this point in
my life, I have met a lot of people who are angry. I've met
more people who get angry when <u>I'm</u> not angry! When anger
goes to the next level, beyond annoyance or being miffed, it is
harmful and destructive. If you come across someone with a
years-long obsession, or worse – rage - watch out. I've been on
the receiving end and it's not pretty. I avoid it now.

The Natural Order of Things

I, middle-aged man, have grown to know myself well enough to know when my life is not in tune with the natural order of things. I know when things are too much of a struggle, at least more than they should be. I know when what I do vocationally and professionally is not in line with my purpose or any type of higher calling. The Universe wants all of us to be self-actualizing individuals. It does not point us in the direction of misery, torture or abuse. It's our responsibility to pick up clues along the way and pay attention to signs we see, feel and experience to position ourselves properly. Once we make the right choices, the tough choices, we reap the benefits, and a universal energy backs us like we haven't felt before to tell us we're going the right way. This is always true.

Appreciate Natural Beauty

I, middle-aged man, bask in and appreciate the beauty of nature and the amazing days it provides. Sometimes, nature is a force, even a deadly one. I'm in awe of its sheer power on one side and its gentleness on the other. I take time to appreciate the changes nature reveals daily and recognize my relatively small place in the world of all living things.

Slow Life Down Sometimes

I, middle-aged man, know that it's an effort to slow my life down but recognize the necessity of doing so. Sometimes, we think that if we slow our lives down amidst the chaos that we will miss something or that something will pass us by. The opposite is true. When we slow down for a short period, it allows our minds to slow down and see things clearly. If we try to spot a deer next to a highway while we're in a car moving 70mph, it would be difficult to see any of its distinguishing characteristics. When the car slows down, it's much easier to see every detail clearly. So it is with life.

Optimism

I, middle-aged man, am positive. I am an optimist. I believe the universe has an order of things and works in my favor even if I can't specifically see how or why yet.

Things Get Toughest the Closer You Are to a Breakthrough

I, middle-aged man, know through experiences in my life that when I am closest to any type of physical, mental or spiritual breakthrough is when things become the most challenging. It is when we are at the final stages of one journey in our lives that our peak seems even farther away. The universal energy tests us most in the final, challenging often painful days or moments. That is when most people lack belief and quit, thinking their time is never going to come.

The Past

I, middle-aged man, am not defined by my past. I'm reminded of this each time someone <u>from</u> my past tries to bring up the parts of my past that were difficult. What defines me is what I'm doing right now, today. I can always restart or rebuild as often as I please.

Worry Another Day

I, middle-aged man, believe that today is the tomorrow I was worried about yesterday.

You Have Nothing to Prove to Anyone Else

I, middle-aged man, have nothing to prove to anyone but myself. With the pressure being released of trying to prove myself to anyone other than myself, I become freed.

Listening to Too Many People

I, middle-aged man, have learned this lesson the hard way: that too many people say too much when you're down and not enough when you're up. Don't listen to too many people either way.

Policy on Disrespect

I, middle-aged man, am aware of how little tolerance I have for disrespect or shade being thrown in my general direction by another person. I don't waste time confronting it or arguing over it. I walk away and let the perpetrator sit in their own shade while I go find some sunlight.

Keep the Promises You Make to Yourself

I, middle-aged man, strive to always keep the promises I make to myself. Sometimes, it's hard. Sometimes, I want to quit on my own promises. But, when I promise myself that I'm going to do something fully and completely and with total commitment, I owe it to myself to follow through on that commitment until it becomes detrimental to me.

Take a Real Vacation

I, middle-aged man, will take a vacation even if it seems I have no time or means to do so. When I was younger and building my career, I used to think it was a sin to take time off. I never took all my time off, and never took actual trips when I unplugged totally from work. I did plenty of travel through work and business to some amazing places, and I figured that was enough travel and exploration. As I got older, the explorer in me has come out. Years ago, I took a memorable trip to Iceland...by myself. It was probably the best trip I've ever taken. If I legitimately don't have time to take a full week off with my family, I will try and find ways to have extended periods unplugged.

Encourage Creativity in Kids

I, middle-aged man, will encourage creativity in my children and other kids in my extended family. I try to remind them of this as often as possible: honing their imaginations and creativity aren't just fun, but they become crucial life skills.

Personal Growth Happens First on the Inside

I, middle-aged man, live by the following mantra: my life can only grow outward in proportion to how strong it is inward. Angels can only find us when they recognize themselves in us.

The Process, not just The Destination

I, middle-aged man, know that the man who loves the process of walking will walk farther than the man who walks solely as a means to get there.

Appreciate Happiness in Others

I, middle-aged man, am genuinely thrilled when I see happiness in other people. I don't forsake others who have happiness, peace, prosperity or clarity in their lives. I make it a point to tell those I'm close with how much I share in their joy whenever possible.

Quiet Moments

I, middle-aged man, make it a point to appreciate the quiet moments in life. A friend from work asked me what all I was planning on doing on my first true day off in a while. I said, "you know, I'm an almost-50-year-old, married, middle-aged man. What do you think I'm going to do?" I got a little bit of sleep. I went through an old baseball card collection that I've had for 35 years. I cleared some debris out of the backyard. I did some errands. Most of all, I breathed. I spent time taking some deep breaths. That's all. It was great.

Pay Attention to Red Flags

I, middle-aged man, am keen to recognize red flags in situations not to judge them but to identify subsequent triggers in myself. I no longer talk myself out of the warnings or cautions I see about a situation, experience, or relationship. Our subconscious "knowing" can and should be trusted at this point in our lives.

Check Up on Loved Ones

I, middle-aged man, vow to do everything possible to check in on loved ones when I know they're going through a rough patch. A kind gesture, call, text or letter goes a long way to helping someone and doesn't take much effort for us to do.

Sometimes, You're Invisible

I, middle-aged man, can handle days when I don't seem seen or heard, or when my opinions or advice aren't taken. It's okay. I let it go. We're not responsible for what other people think, only what we think.

Anniversaries Matter. Don't Forget Them.

I, middle-aged man, know that anniversaries matter to most people, including myself. We don't have to do elaborate celebrations for them, but we do need to honor them even briefly. They mark an important passage of time and often mark milestones in our lives. These occasions deserve to have our respect.

Ancient Wisdom

I, middle-aged man, believe that "when your cup is full, stop pouring."

– Lao Tzu

Reflect on Your Own Childhood, Briefly

I, middle-aged man, know that sometimes we get the opportunity to see or read things from our early childhood. With my mom's passing, I saw a folder of things she had kept for over 40 years. Most of them are things I had long forgotten about, like things I wrote in 2nd grade or 3rd grade. The thing that struck me about reading my little poems and other things I was quoting at the time was how little I've changed. I quoted Lao Tzu in one of my writing assignments...in 3rd grade. So that hasn't changed. I am fully aware, however, of how little value there really is in some of these old items to anyone else but me. They're just fond memories now, but still important ones.

Believe in Your Own Abilities

I, middle-aged man, know that not everyone is religious, nor do I preach that anyone should be. Still, we can live by relevant bits of wisdom even if we're not religious:

"Even the least among you can do all that I have done, and even greater."

- John, 14:12

Practice Patience

I, middle-aged man, practice a patient mindset in my life and try to do an even better job exercising it when possible. Things seem to naturally unfold for the patient man. Like the Wise Farmer, we cannot possibly know what lies in store for us, or the timetable in which things will occur. We must use patience to see how things fully develop.

This Too Shall Pass

I, middle-aged man, commit to living by this mantra: whatever is going on in our lives, <u>this too shall pass</u>. The older and wiser I get, the more this statement holds real gravitas. When things are good – "too good", on top of the world, the smartest person in the room – this too shall pass. When things are bad – horrible day, everything going wrong, terrible luck that never seems to end – this too shall pass. You're never as good as your very best day, but you're never as bad as your very worst day.

Really, Stop Complaining

I, middle-aged man, recognize that sometimes, we just must do things without complaint and questions asked. When this is necessary, I shut my mouth, take care of my business, don't complain about it, and take care of my shit. I don't drag others down or bring people into the things that I am responsible for. It has nothing to do with being anti-social or withholding my feelings. It is about facing life head-on with no fear, bellyaching or martyrdom.

No More Second-Guessing

I, middle-aged man, no longer second-guess myself and my decisions. If I'm asked my opinion on something, it's for a reason: I've earned it, or others thought highly enough of me to ask. If I'm a subject matter <u>expert</u> on something, I don't second guess the knowledge I've gained and the work it took to become that expert. If my subconscious is telling me to act or react one way in a certain situation, I believe it.

Plant Trees that Provide Shade

I, middle-aged man, remind myself of an old saying that very simply describes what real, unconditional kindness, consideration and forward-thinking means: "a true virtue of life is to plant trees under whose shade you do not expect to sit."

Bridges

I, middle-aged man, appreciate this quote:

"The hardest thing to learn in life is which bridges to cross and which to burn."

- Bertrand Russell

Become Educated About Narcissism and Narcissistic Abuse

I, middle-aged man, vow to continue to be as educated as possible about all forms of narcissism, narcissistic personality disorder (NPD), and the dangers to its victims, so I can teach educate future generations. I believe there is an epidemic of narcissism in the world today that I must help to unmask. Narcissism doesn't mean someone's "batshit crazy". That may be true, but there's much more to it than that, too. I commit to continue studying these disorders, helping inform other men and women about not falling victim to them, and what to do if it happens.

Find Purpose in Service

I, middle-aged man, believe my best days happen when I'm of service to others. I make it a point to carry out acts of service when possible whether it includes mentoring someone, giving someone advice, being a listening ear or taking the trash out. With each act of service, it makes my personal foundation stronger and my capacity to understand the human condition more enlightened.

Pay <u>Daily</u> Attention to Your Health

I, middle-aged man, recognize the importance of my health not only on days when I don't feel my best. I understand that by the time I don't feel well, it's likely too late to avoid illness. I commit to being in tune with my body and mind and not denying when something isn't quite right. I take the necessary precautions to address it if needed.

I

I, middle-aged man, approach life in a kind-hearted way.

Become a "No-Limit" Person

I, middle-aged man, recognize the upside of trying to raise my personal ceiling towards becoming a "no-limit" person. A no-limit person has no cap on what they're able to accomplish. They're not held back by any preconceived notions, what other people think, or by their own rigidity. The no-limit person embraces freedom of thought, passion, exploration and principle.

Being Alone isn't Being Lonely

I, middle-aged man, believe this:

"All of man's troubles derive from not being able to sit quietly in a room alone."

- Blaise Pascal

Power

"Amateurs chase the sun and get burned. Power stays in the shadows."

- "Oppenheimer"

365 Days of Resolutions

I, middle-aged man, do not believe in New Year's resolutions. I don't believe that there's only one day a year that we can make resolutions for ourselves, or change a pattern we've been in. An entire year is made up of 365 equal parts we call days. I can choose to restart or change directions on any one of those days and do not need a special occasion to mark a change in perspective or action.

Fulfillment in "Things"

I, middle-aged man, am aware that I'm less interested in big, flashy, price-taggy things. The fancy cars. The status. The cool apartment. The clothing that showed off who I aspired to be even if that was divergent from who I was. All those things matter less as I get older. It's in fact the less flashy things that matter a lot <u>more</u> now. The kind, handwritten letter. The thoughtful email. The photos. The in-person experiences. The long-lost friends. The new friends. If I find myself being drawn to the less tangible, less flashy things in life, I know I'm on the right path. Yes, I still appreciate nice things. No, it's not how I derive fulfillment.

Refresh Your Perspective Often

I, middle-aged man, believe that there are many opportunities for me to refresh my perspective on life or aspects of it. It is not too late to unapologetically change, reverse, sidestep, or start totally over on something.

Ask the Universe

I, middle-aged man, don't hesitate to ask the Universe for what I need. I ask earnestly and with a full heart, but not desperately. Once I do, I act as if what I've asked for is on its way to me already. By doing so, I summon the power of attraction and manifestation.

Feeling Your Age

I, middle-aged man, give myself a pass on days that I may feel my age. I know that there's probably a reason that not many 50-year-old's have small children, unless there's a live-in nanny or people around the home who don't work. I give myself permission to feel completely exhausted and tired occasionally. It's okay. I try and make sure to recharge fast, though.

What You Focus On is What You'll See (and Get)

I, middle-aged man, know that if I focus on obstacles or obstructions, all I will see are obstacles or obstructions. Everything I put my focus on in life, good or bad, becomes magnified. If I focus on a lot of little things that are going wrong, I'll magnify them into bigger things than they would have been otherwise. Our minds know how to focus but don't distinguish between good and bad outcomes. It's up to me to choose to focus on things in order to magnify the results I want and to manifest what I want versus what I don't want. Wherever I place my focus, my body and actions always naturally follow.

Choose Optimism

I, middle-aged man, have little utility for pessimism. If something isn't right, it's either under my control to fix or it's not. I avoid mindless complaining or brain dumps about things that restrict my movement forward. If my mind is negative or cluttered and I need to clear it, the solution is found within the resources I know like meditation and self-reflection.

Aim for Self-Actualization

I, middle-aged man, commit to a life of self-actualizing. It's been observed that the traits of self-actualizers include an appreciation for beauty, a sense of purpose, resistance to enculturation, welcoming the unknown, high enthusiasm, inner directedness, detachment from outcome, independence of the good opinion of others, and absence of a compelling need to exert control over others.

One famous example of what it means to self-actualize was part of a Masters-level research study and included one question to the students in the study: "A fully self-actualized person arrives at a dinner party at which everyone is dressed in formal attire. He is wearing blue jeans, a t-shirt, sneakers and a ball cap. What does he think and what does he do? You have thirty minutes to write your answer."

The answers given by the students were similar: they mostly answered that the self-actualized person would feel a higher mission and sense of purpose around his clothing choices. Some said it was that the self-actualized person wanted to make a statement in his clothing choice. Some said it was simply a direct choice to be different from everyone else.

The professor then informed the participants that they all failed the assignment. The correct answer was simply," he wouldn't notice." To a self-actualized person, comparing one's clothing choices to other people's choices is a totally unnecessary mental exercise. He wouldn't even contemplate it.

High and Low Expectations

I, middle-aged man, have high expectations for myself. I have low expectations for everyone else. This is how I "level up." I keep my standards high, my tolerance for low standards low, and gravitate towards better more positive energy consistently. I will naturally drift from those who act poorly and instead surround myself with people that share my principles and energy who are more closely aligned with mine.

Relating to Different Generations

I, middle-aged man, commit to not forming my ideologies based solely on my own generation. I seek to better understand other generations before and after me. I am not, however, compelled to <u>agree</u> with other generations or pretend to identify with them. I simply vow to try and better understand them so I can better relate to my kids, grandkids someday and those who will carry the torch going forward.

Not Losing Yourself

I, middle-aged man, realize that the most significant person I've ever lost was me. I love other people including family and friends. But the deepest love I must possess is for myself. I didn't always understand that, but now I do. I wouldn't have it any other way. "Be forever an egomaniac" is <u>not</u> what I'm saying. Loving oneself is a higher calling than artificially self-proclaiming your dominance over another.

Two Lives, not Nine

I, middle-aged man, believe everyone has two lives. The second one starts the minute we realize we have only one.

Know When to Speak

I, middle-aged man, don't air out all my feelings. There is wisdom in knowing when to speak and when not to. A fool will vent all his feelings all the time. A wise man holds them back.

When to Walk Away from a Challenge

I, middle-aged man, believe that there will be a time when it makes sense to walk away from certain challenges we face. If I already have a lifetime of battle scars, it's hardly quitting. It's called choosing your battles. It's the secret to longevity.

Taking Care of the Kids

I, middle-aged man, know that no matter what choices I make for myself, I must make sure my children are provided for short and long-term. That's the number one goal as a parent in middle-aged: to ensure our children are set up to have better lives as adults than we had. I can take all the advice I want about how to better my own life in middle age, but my commitment to my children even when they're grown adults is always a priority.

Imperfection

I, middle-aged man, commit to reading and re-reading the following quote:

"The student should constantly look within his human self, and see what habits or creations are there that need to be plucked out and disposed of. For only by refusing to any longer allow habits of judging, condemning and criticizing to exist, can he be free. The true activity of the student is only to perfect his own world and he cannot do it if he sees imperfection in the world or in anyone else."

- Tilopa

Goals and Process

I, middle-aged man, believe that any goal we attain is not the source of our joy. The amount of effort, struggle and progress (or process) needed in attaining a goal drives the degree to which we experience joy when the goal is reached. This is an absolute truth in life.

As a Result, Set Very High Goals

I, middle-aged man, believe we are in an epidemic of setting low or no goals, which is therefore creating less joy in the world. If our goal is to clean out the garage, take out the trash, do our taxes, and do our laundry this week, these are all fine things to do. In any week, we might accomplish these very easy and mindless tasks, and might also experience very little joy as a result. It's because tasks or task lists don't constitute real goals because there is no real process involved in doing them. If the goal is to run a marathon, that would be a fine goal. You would have months of training and learning about the intricacies of your body and how it recovers from strenuous activity. Then, you run the race and finish. The amount of joy you feel is enormous. The source of joy is not that you ran the marathon…millions of people have too. It was <u>your</u> specific journey, <u>your</u> progress, and overcoming <u>your</u> obstacles in running the marathon that makes it so joyful.

Walk Away

I, middle-aged man, know by now that if people aren't listening to us, we should probably stop talking to them.

Uncaused Joy

I, middle-aged man, hold "uncaused joy" in high regard. This type of joy speaks to our inherent inner core, either through days or years of work through re-engineering our minds or the very essence we're born with. What the phrase means is that we're able to achieve and feel deep and lasting joy unrelated to outside forces or things. On a small scale, if you are walking down a city street and see a $5 bill on the sidewalk that appears to be unclaimed, you feel the immediate joy of it being your lucky day. Pretty soon, though, you forget about this $5 gift. On a large scale, when I win the Powerball jackpot, I will feel immediate joy and it might last quite a bit longer than if I found $5 on the sidewalk. Still, eventually, the joy caused by that event will fade, too. In both cases, there are external factors causing our burst of joy. It's not joy that is built-in or pre-wired in our being, so it doesn't last.

Expecting Kindness in Return

I, middle-aged man, know that if we practice kindness, it's nice to get it in return. But we don't expect it. If we don't get it, that's okay, we move on and aren't bummed about it. Kindness isn't supposed to be transactional.

Outcomes

I, middle-aged man, have realized that most people live life needing to know an outcome before something starts. They try to outthink the Universe. They forget how powerless they really are, and believe they have control over the uncontrollable. What happened to wanting mystery or suspense, and feeling confident we can handle whatever the outcome is? Knowing too much about the past and trying too much to have advanced knowledge of the future causes suffering and disappointment. We stick to what we're doing now and whatever the outcomes are we will always be able to handle them.

Be Like a River

I, middle-aged man, admire the qualities of a river which I try and emulate. It stays low, runs powerfully yet smoothly, adapts to its surrounding conditions, and changes courses easily and without difficulty. The ground around it is fertile and all life flows towards it. Eventually, it breaks free from its basin and opens up into a vaster body of water.

Listening

I, middle-aged man, understand that when we know the most, we must listen the most.

Take a Hike

I, middle-aged man, commit to consistently going outside to take a hike no matter what physical condition I might be in on any given day. There is nothing like being outside immersed in nature at every opportunity. The therapeutic and mind-clearing benefits are real.

Teach Your Kids What You Know

I, middle-aged man, embrace the things I know and the talents I have. I commit to never forgetting about them. Not so I can relive my glory days, but so that I can pass these skills onto my children.

Know Your Ancestry

I, middle-aged man, make it a point to do my own detective work about my family's roots and heritage. It's part of my responsibility to inform people that come after me about the people who came before me.

Buyer Beware

I, middle-aged man, live by the mantra "buyer always beware."
Do your research fully and completely on every single aspect
before making any big purchase, big decision, or forming a
partnership. Leave no stone unturned when it comes to
understanding anything you're getting yourself into legally or
even on a handshake agreement. Uncover every stone possible.

Offering Help That's Not Taken

I, middle-aged man, will always try and offer help when I feel I can be helpful. If I'm offering help and it's not taken, I must stop offering. Same thing goes for offering advice, wisdom and perspective.

Moving Couches

I, middle-aged man, remind myself that two people can move a couch quite easily. One person, alone, struggles. And so it is with partnerships, businesses and relationships. They're only hard when one person is trying to do the work that's made for two people.

What You Control, and What You Don't

I, middle-aged man, contemplate the topic of control. I used to believe that I could control anything I set my mind to. That not only could I control the outcomes of things, but I could control the very process it took to create those outcomes. The thinking when I was younger was that the more I can control people, the more powerful I could be, and the more outcomes would be in my favor. I couldn't have been more wrong about that. It's the total opposite. But make no mistake; we still have many, many choices in life. Our power of thought, action and behavior are our powers, no one or no force can take them from us.

Be Aware of Your Own Trauma

I, middle-aged man, recognize that what we learn and become accustomed to at a young age is extremely difficult to alter later in life. If we're accustomed to being in a toxic and abusive environment over many years, we'll be more apt to recreate that same environment for others. It takes a lot of awareness and enlightenment to break whatever patterns have turned into default behaviors or emotions over a long period of time. The cycle is only broken if we decide we're going to do whatever it takes to break the cycle.

High Levels of Self-Awareness

I, middle-aged man, commit to operating with a high level of self-awareness. I trust myself, love myself, and listen to myself. But I'm aware of the effect my words, actions and behaviors can have on others.

Using All of Your Time to Its Fullest

I, middle-aged man, am mindful of my time. I know that as I age, time is my most valuable currency. In almost every decision I make, there is a time/value calculation going on in my head. No matter what the price, I make sure I have enough time to do what I feel I need to do.

Welcome High-Vibration People

I, middle-aged man, am committed to meeting new, fascinating, high-vibration people across all walks of life. Connecting with people I find interesting who have a different perspective than me and are kind feeds my energy. At work, I naturally gravitate towards these types of people and vice versa. In personal circles, same thing.

Stay True to Your Principles

I, middle-aged man, am not afraid to ruffle a few feathers if need be. Defending my principles, ideas, and beliefs necessitates that. When I'm doing so, the people who feel most threatened will always lash back at me the greatest. Those who aren't threatened and are content in who they are never will. It's a good way to tell if I'm in the right, non-toxic crowd. Even if I'm not, I still don't back away from my core beliefs.

You're Less of a Work in Progress than You Think

I, middle-aged man, have worked very hard up to this point in my life to be able to say: I'm no longer a "work in progress". I am tired of having been a work in progress for so long. So, now, what you get is what you get with me. I'm happy with exactly who I am, and don't wish to uncover past traumas or travel ground already passed over. Whatever's behind me is behind me, and I've lived several lives already and iterated each time. I'm about as close to a finished product as I will be, and I'm good with that.

Travel Light

I, middle-aged man, pack light and travel light, bringing only what I need with me. I try not to get weighed down with things I don't definitively need. It's a metaphor for my life.

I Am

I, middle-aged man, am a nature lover and animal lover. A lover of pets, gardens, flowers, wild animals, oceans, trees, forests, soil, mountains, and the beach. Anything that carries with it the essence of life, I love.

That <u>One</u> Day

I, middle-aged man, will be able to identify that there will be one day when a major shift in our life is happening or is supposed to happen. That feeling of shifting will happen probably multiple times in our lives. I'll just know when it does. I'll feel an energetic shift and positive momentum moving me out of a current situation and into a new one. I will trust it and won't question it.

Don't Hang On; Let Go

I, middle-aged man, vow to not hang on too tightly for too long to any one thing or possession. The tighter I hang onto certain things or possessions, the weaker my grip becomes in a shorter period of time.

The Why

I, middle-aged man, believe that he who has a why can bear
almost any how.

Special Moments

I, middle-aged man, know how to cherish special moments. When my daughter talks about our weekend together at her school's "show and tell" day, there's no replacement for that. Or when my son says "Dada", there's no replacement for that. Anything else I've done or accomplished in this lifetime seems meaningless in comparison to the special moments that can't be reproduced.

Handling Regrets

I, middle-aged man, don't ask myself if I would go back and change anything about my life. I wouldn't. I don't let my mind store regrets. I realize and accept that I am, right now, the sum of everything that has happened to this point. The Universe always has an underlying reason for everything. The only things I can do are to choose how I look at things today and accept everything that's already happened.

Physical Health Challenges

I, middle-aged man, know that physical health challenges are "right now" challenges for me. In other words, I deal with them right now if there's a problem. We all have some level of genetic predisposition to disease, ailments or certain conditions. But I know that taking care of all aspects of my health are day-in and day-out commitments I must make.

Self-Control

I, middle-aged man, know that some of the greatest men in history, like Marcus Aurelius, Epictetus, and Seneca, have acted in accordance with a specific philosophy. It's not only a system, but a foundation for life. A necessity, in fact, rooted in a stoic mindset of logic and naturalistic ethics. In practice, it means the development of self-control and fortitude to overcome destructive emotions. It means becoming a clear and unbiased thinker, thereby understanding universal reason. Stoicism's primary characteristic derives from improving the individual's ethical and moral well-being in order to align with Nature. It applies to interpersonal relationships (which resembles the teachings of Alfred Adler, the noted Psychologist), that are free from anger, envy and jealousy, and to accept even the downtrodden as equals of other men because all men are products of nature.

Why does this all matter, especially to middle-aged men? Because who amongst us couldn't use a little bit more self-control, acceptance, and emotional regulation? No matter what happens around us or to us, we can accept it, live with it and thrive under it. It's not as if we are figuratively wearing protective armor by not letting anything into our psyches. It's, in fact, the opposite. We're letting <u>everything</u> around us in and taking it all in stride. The difference is that we can handle it; and not only handle it, thrive amidst it. We're in a sense able to believe that no matter what happens, we carry with us the quiet confidence that we are acting in accordance with nature and our own moral code of conduct that we believe in deeply.

You're Not Overwhelmed

I, middle-aged man, am never overwhelmed even if
conventional wisdom might say I am. The Universe will never,
ever put us in a situation we cannot handle. If we're faced with
difficulty, it's because a greater being or force knows we can
get through it even if we don't yet believe it. The fact that we
are put into multiple complex situations seemingly at the same
time means we're doing something exactly right and exactly
aligned with what nature has in store for us based on what we
can handle.

Leading Others

I, middle-aged man, commit to becoming a better leader without forcing my individual style upon anyone. I, in turn, study other people's leadership styles in order to help refine my own. All a great leader or coach does is set the environment for other people's success and turns them loose. To do anything but that is a disservice to others and hurts, or at least inhibits, the team's performance.

There are some leadership and management <u>principles</u> (honesty, transparency, empowerment, accountability) that always hold true and stand the test of time. There are some leadership and management <u>styles</u>, however, that evolve every half-generation or so. If we have a career for 40 years, we're probably having to adapt our style 3 or 4 times in our life to be an effective leader.

Lastly, if we always believe that as a leader, we're the smartest person in the room, most of the time we'll be wrong. Remember, there is always someone, somewhere in the world, who probably is smarter than us on any given day.

Don't Take Too Many People's Advice

I, middle-aged man, will not take advice from too many people at this stage in my life. In fact, the fewer the better. Leave behind the days of checking with anyone to "make sure it's ok", or seeking counsel from people we don't know, trust or respect. We are way past that point in our lives when we must second-guess our instincts or listen to other people telling us we're wrong when most of the time we know we're right. We stop short of letting people talk us out of what we <u>know</u> is our own truth.

Understand Gaslighting

I, middle-aged man, will better know and understand the word gaslighting. I wrote an entire book about this topic called *Above the Fog* based loosely on my own personal experiences with a malignant narcissist. What is gaslighting exactly? It's a form of psychological manipulation in which the abuser attempts to sow self-doubt and confusion in their victim's mind through lies and misdirection. Typically, gaslighters seek to gain power and control over another person by distorting reality and forcing them to question their own judgment and intuition. Mild instances of gaslighting may happen to us and we shrug them off. Chronic gaslighting and the dangers from it are very serious. It's dished out typically by a very disturbed individual who makes it a habit of truth-bending and distortion of the facts and reality of a serious nature. We must put a very strong barrier up between us and people who attempt to gaslight us. Don't engage with them, don't listen to them, and don't hang around with them.

Fail, Learn and Move on

I, middle-aged man, know that if I do something wrong, make an incorrect decision or don't meet the standard I set for myself, not to dwell on it (or <u>in</u> it). I take what I need from the experience and put it quickly behind me. We fail fast, learn faster and move on even faster.

Embrace Inspiration, However Small

I, middle-aged man, am aware of the times when I'm totally uninspired and not "feeling it." Some days, nothing meets the expectations that I set for myself. Everything and everybody seem to disappoint; and if not disappoint, they do nothing to inspire positivity, optimism, much less confidence. Have we had days like these? Sometimes, we must look for and find the smallest possible silver linings. It could be in a single kind word, a positive thought, nice weather, a friendly glance, or an inspirational quote from someone. Do something, or put yourself in a situation, to find a silver lining.

Each Day, A Gift

I, middle-aged man, know there's a reason they call it the "present". Today's a gift.

The Time to Act is Now

I, middle-aged man, believe that if we're wondering when we should act on something, the answer could be now. Today may be it.

Belief from Experience

I, middle-aged man, believe nothing unless I experience it to be true firsthand. When my dad says "I love you" to me, I believe him. I believe him because he backs it up based on how he treats me, and what my own first-hand experience is. However, if someone makes an assertion that's not backed up by their actions, I won't believe it until I know it to be true firsthand.

Teamwork

I, middle-aged man, understand the importance of partnerships and teamwork. I know that no matter how much I improve my own perspective and mentality in order to take pride in some level of independence, inevitably I will need to rely on the cooperation with others. This extends to personal relationships, professional relationships and even encounters with strangers. The degree to which I make those interactions pleasant, the more likely it is that trust will be built, and the better teamwork will be long-term. Trust is the building block, though.

Be Ready

I, middle-aged man, am ready for whatever is next in my life. Everything I've done to this point is enough to give me the confidence that I can handle any life situation even if it seems scary, painful or new.

When to Compromise, When to Fight

I, middle-aged man, know the vital importance of two life skills: the art of compromise, and the art of knowing what battles are worth fighting greatly for. We probably know a little bit about both at this point, and refining those skills pay off big time for our health and success. Why? Because so few people know how to operate in a world that has only a little bit of compromise in it.

A fool will fight every single battle presented to him and eventually becomes drained. A wise man fights only the battles he chooses on his terms, and lives to see many more days.

You'll Disappoint Some People. So, What Else is New?

I, middle-aged man, understand that I'm bound to disappoint some people. Most of the time, it is unintentional. But life experiences have taught me that when I don't do things the way other people want me to, they're naturally disappointed. There is nothing wrong with this. When I follow what I believe is my truth, there will be people who get naturally moved out of the way. They will be disappointed because we're not acting how we have in the past or how they want us to in the present. We can't please everyone, nor should we try. Our people will always be our people if we are making an honest effort.

Change the Rules When Necessary

I, middle-aged man, understand that when someone changes the game on us, we sometimes must respond by changing our own game. It's most likely a necessity. Too often, someone changes the game on us in a professional setting or in a relationship, and then that very same someone reacts negatively when we stand up for ourselves or change our terms of engagement in response.

All we can do is unapologetically adapt to any given situation we're in or get put in. We can't apologize for that. Sometimes we must adapt to changing circumstances in the interests of our own health, survival, well-being or self-actualization. There can be no sacrifices for those things.

Set Boundaries for Your Own Needs, Too

I, middle-aged man, need to be a little more selfish today, with my time, love, resources, and bandwidth. It's okay to be a little more selfish than we think we are. Most of us tend to err on the side of being too <u>unselfish</u>. Our own pride too often cautions us against doing anything that would feel to us as selfish or be seen by others as selfish. We favor others' needs over our own <u>a lot.</u>

In the long run, we'll be glad we started to treat ourselves with at least as much attention than we do other people. It's like the say in the announcements after boarding an airplane: put on your own oxygen masks before you help others. Otherwise, you're no good to anyone else.

Accept the Days When Life Kicks You in the Teeth

I, middle-aged man, accept the fact that some days I really do get kicked in the teeth by life and I must suck it up and trudge through it. It's a part of life when this happens. When I consider that my time here is transient, nothing is permanent, and therefore the daily challenges I face aren't either, it makes the choice to accept these days (or laugh at them) easier.

Charitable Giving

I, middle-aged man, believe it is important to find causes that are important to me that I can commit to supporting financially or through volunteer work. Doing so reenforces that I'm a small part of something much bigger, and that this world isn't at all about me.

How You Look at Things

I, middle-aged man, know that when you change the way you look at things, the things you look at change.

It's one of the great lines uttered by Dr. Wayne Dyer. If we look at something and change our perspective on what it is we're looking at, it changes. It morphs. It isn't how it may have first appeared to us. We can change the entire energy around something if we want to, which then changes how our mind's eye views that problem.

The "Three S" Trifecta

I, middle-aged man, aim for sweat, sun and silence each day.
Try it.

More is Usually Less, Except...

I, middle-aged man, have known firsthand that sometimes having more turns out to result in less. In fact, most of the time this is true. More money, more problems. Possessions? No, because those are impermanent. Accomplishments? No, because then we must listen too much to other people's expectations. We don't need more accomplishments.

The only thing where more is truly more is time.

Avoid Confrontation when Emotions are Running Hot

I, middle-aged man, know that I'm at my worst when emotions are running high and I'm not able to slow down and think rationally. I do everything possible to avoid a fight or confrontation when emotions run high. I do all things possible to walk away, or let the situation calm down.

Not Every Lesson is Ours

I, middle-aged man, know that not every lesson in life is ours to learn anymore.

Past Wounds

I, middle-aged man, try to not let any past wounds I have bleed on the very people who had nothing to do with how I got cut.

Mom's

I, middle-aged man, believe it is important for all of us to honor our mom's. No matter what our story or relationship is with mom, whether alive, deceased, estranged or simply just strange, we take time to honor our mom's and all the other mom's we know of in our lives. They're important and special no matter what.

A Mirror or Sponge?

I, middle-aged man, know the importance, when it comes to dealing with others, to consider whether to be a mirror or a sponge. How much do we want to absorb versus bounce right back at them? What kind of energy serves us better to accept rather than deflect back? Sometimes, it's necessary to be a mirror so other people know and see exactly how they are treating us – good or bad. Sometimes, it's necessary to simply listen and be a sponge for someone else.

Always Choose Our Strengths over Weaknesses

I, middle-aged man, commit to spending more time embracing and using my strengths and much less time focused on my supposed weaknesses or shortcomings. At this point in life, I can go a lot farther on my strengths than I can spending time even thinking about my weaknesses.

"I Am" Statement

I, middle-aged man, am better than I sometimes think I am.

Level Up

I, middle-aged man, live to level up each day. I commit to raising the bar for myself as often as necessary. I commit to doing things with like-minded people. I commit to always having a career or trade that pays me what I am worth or what the market commands. I commit to spending more time with people I have things in common with. I commit to lovingly welcoming my children always closer to me especially when they are having difficulties.

Making Hard Choices

I, middle-aged man, commit to not backing down from making hard choices. We no doubt have faced hard choices to this point and will face more of them. Things like stepping away from people or projects. Truly knowing when it's okay to let go, and when it's maybe better to hang on a little longer. When to distance ourselves from people. When or how to move on from your job or career. Knowing when it's okay to disappoint someone else if you don't disappoint yourself.

These are not problems, they're choices. And some choices are harder than others. We're in the period of our lives when making hard choices that others aren't equipped to make is a necessity if not a rite of passage. We embrace the discomfort. We understand that we will never be faced with a choice that we can't make. The world has prepared us for tough choices. If we haven't had to make any yet, we will.

Starting Over 101

I, middle-aged man, know that if I must start aspects of my life over, I will start over enthusiastically. I know from experience that's it's never too late to start anything over again. If need be, I let go of my old identity, old friends, old acquaintances, and old memories that no longer serve me. I don't rely on them any longer. I cut the cord from all things that were destructive. I let past experiences speak for themselves, and commit to forging new relationships, experiences and ways of living.

Starting Over 102

I, middle-aged man, know that new beginnings in any area of my life requires two things: incredible confidence and incredible faith. There is a damn good reason why so many people are afraid of new beginnings in middle age. It's hard. There are gut checks along the way. There are easy reasons <u>not</u> to start over, and easy ways out. This is why confidence and faith are the two most important ingredients. We must listen to and believe in ourselves. No matter what anyone tells us, we can do it. In some cases – ones that involve abuse, manipulation, assault, mistreatment or downright misery – we <u>must</u> restart out of survival. We get one shot at life, but along the way we get multiple shots at starting over. Take all of them.

50% More

I, middle-aged man, know that to become self-actualized – to truly know my potential and meet it – and to live the life I've always imagined, I must have 50% more belief in myself than the person closest to me does. That's the cost of self-improvement.

Self-Development Doesn't Have to Stop

I, middle-aged man, commit to continuously working on myself and my physical, emotional and spiritual development from this day forward. I know that it is possible to have new personal bests in life each day.

About The Truth

I, middle-aged man, have learned that the truth always comes out even if it takes a while. The Universe has a particular way of revealing the truth, or having the truth unfold, at the exact right time and place.

Recalibrate Your Purpose Consistently

I, middle-aged man, know that when work or professional decisions come up, I need to make sure they're aligned with my purpose. I can't sacrifice what I believe my purpose to be for a safe paycheck. I know that the meaning of life is whatever I determine it to be. I must constantly be evaluating my work and personal progress against what purpose is on any given day.

Stop! Be Present

I, middle-aged man, will stop what I'm doing right now. I will be in the moment, right now, giving total attention to my thoughts, ideas, feelings and emotions. I will sit with them for one minute without judgment. And I commit to practicing this once a week until it becomes more frequent.

Water Your Plants, Tend to the Roots

I, middle-aged man, understand the metaphor of taking care of my plants and giving them plenty of water and nourishment, exactly the way I should nourish my own life and my own soul.

Set an Example of Calm

I, middle-aged man, commit to practicing calmness in my own life so that I may be an example to others to keep peace amidst chaos. The best things we can do for people are two-fold: one, not sugarcoating reality; and two, embracing a way of calmness, confidence and optimism.

Staying Physically Fit

I, middle-aged man, commit to a life of physical well-being and fitness. Remember those days when we were teenagers? Early 20's? Even 30's? We were spry. We were flexible. We were strong. We could eat whatever we wanted with little or no consequences. We had stamina, energy, vitality. We felt in command of our health.

Then, something happened. We slowed down. We got sick. We sat for too many hours in a chair. We traded outdoor sunlight for indoor fluorescent lighting. We weren't jumping out of bed so quickly, and if we did, we probably pulled something.

Even as we age, though, our bodies want to get to a natural and healthy state. When we take some time off from being physically active and then come back that first time, we're exhausted and sore, right? It's our bodies shaking off the cobwebs. It's not our body telling us to stop, quit or that it was a bad idea to start working out. It's a good sign.

Marvel at Beautiful Days

I, middle-aged man, still marvel at the beautiful days outside the same way I did when I was a kid, when I was dreaming of endless hours spent playing games in the yard or in the woods with friends. It's a reminder that there's a lot to be grateful for and sometimes we only need to open a window or take a step outside to benefit from it. It's why one of the anecdotes to feeling bummed out is to get up and go outside.

Speak With Purpose or Not at All

I, middle-aged man, embrace the notion that the older we get, the quieter we become. There is less of a need to make a point or have our voices heard simply to be heard. We have less of a need to react and more of a desire to contemplate and reflect. When we do speak, it should speak volumes.

Slow Down & Hit "Pause" If You Must

I, middle-aged man, will allow myself to take my time today and be a bit more deliberate. Being more deliberate gives me more presence of mind in what I'm doing. Whatever it is we're in a hurry for, we'll take our time. Pause. Reflect. Relax. See what happens if we just take the day today and wait without reacting.

Negative Emotions Have Their Place, Too

I, middle-aged man, know there's no possible way to squelch every single negative thought that comes into my mind. I give myself permission to allow those negative feelings and emotions to exist for a short while. If we're aware of those negative thoughts, it means we're more spiritually advanced and tuned in to our emotions than most people. Most people who don't realize when they're being negative blame their mood on every other factor around them except what's going on inside of them. We'll bounce back sooner if we allow these emotions for a short time.

Your "Ex-anything"

I, middle-aged man, fully understand that our "Ex-anything" ... wife, boss, lover, friend ... are called "Ex" for very good reason. At one point in the distant past, they might have served us well. Then, they didn't. And now, they don't know anything about us anymore because we're different. Sometimes, Ex's try and haunt us and stay with us. They do bad things like call us names or try and send trauma back in our direction. Don't let them. Don't look back, don't turn back, and don't even pause when faced with an Ex-anything. Stay on your path.

Little Gifts

I, middle-aged man, reserve places in my heart for the joy and gratitude in little things and little moments. To see the joy on my daughters' faces as they open a box of gifts that I gave them is priceless. To hear my son uttering his first words is priceless. I'm so grateful to share little moments such as those. The littlest gifts can be enormous.

Practice Random Acts of Kindness

I, middle-aged man, gravitate towards random and unsolicited acts of kindness. I notice them. I try to practice them. I appreciate seeing others practice them.

It's All in How You Handle Stuff

I, middle-aged man, believe that so much of how I go through life comes down to how I handle the things that don't go the way I want them to. I know it's not about what challenges I face, but how I deal with them. It's a choice between bravery and truth or cowardice, excuses and denial.

Maslow's Hammer

I, middle-aged man, am consistently working on becoming more versatile in my perspectives, relationships, social interactions and skills. I treat versatility as an ongoing commitment to improvement and becoming better as a person and professional.

"It is tempting, if the only tool you have is a hammer, to treat everything as if it were a nail."

- Abraham Maslow

What Other People Think

I, middle-aged man, don't care what other people think about me. I know that if I have good intentions and am pleasant to people, my interactions with others will be positive. I cannot control, nor do I wish to control, how other people choose to respond to me or think of me.

Mistakes

I, middle-aged man, have made a ton of mistakes in my life and continue to make them. When I fail, I fail fast and sometimes spectacularly. I choose not to harp on things for too long and not to dwell in the negative outcomes for too long. I choose to learn from my mistakes and move on with no guilt, shame or emotions that weigh me down. It's not my intention, but I'm not afraid of making mistakes.

Self-Inflicted Suffering

I, middle-aged man, believe that a great degree of the suffering I dealt with in the past was self-inflicted. When something wasn't perfect or the way I wanted it to be in my eyes, the initial thought was that I was getting a raw deal. Not only is this immature, but it's incredibly unenlightened. I now know better and am aware not to allow self-inflicted suffering.

Dad's

I, middle-aged man, honor all the other Dad's out there and feel a kinship to them. I have very little expectation or need for fanfare or elaborate celebrations as a Dad. If we're fortunate enough to have those around us truly celebrate us and make a big deal about Father's Day or birthdays, wonderful! If not, don't fret. Honor our own Dad's, whether here or departed, whether he treated us well or poorly. Know in our heart of hearts how valuable Dad's are to someone else. Take a minute to thank our own Dad's in our own way. For better or worse, they've taught us lessons we can choose to emulate or not.

When Friends Pass Away

I, middle-aged man, understand and accept the emotions we face when things start happening to our friends. It's one thing as we get older to witness aging of grandparents and parents, and their contemporaries. As a younger person, we grow up expecting that. Most of us are not prepared for the suddenness of losing a friend or relative that is our age. Why? Because that means our time could be right around the corner too! If tomorrow's the day we're gone off the earth, so be it. It's been a great run. I've done my best.

Chapters of Life

I, middle-aged man, relate to something written by Portia Nelson, as follows, about the various stages of life and lessons learned:

- ✓ "Chapter 1: I walk down the street. There is a deep hole in the sidewalk. I fall in. I am lost...I am helpless. It isn't my fault. It takes me forever to find a way out.

- ✓ Chapter 2: I walk down the street. There is a deep hole in the sidewalk. I pretend I don't see it. I fall in again. I can't believe I am in the same place, but it isn't my fault. It still takes a long time to get out.

- ✓ Chapter 3: I walk down the street. There is a deep hole in the sidewalk. I see it is there. I still fall in...it's a habit. My eyes are open. I know where I am. It is my fault. I get out immediately.

- ✓ Chapter 4: I walk down the same street. There is a deep hole in the sidewalk. I walk around it.

- ✓ Chapter 5: I walk down another street."

Trust What You've Learned

I, middle-aged man, give thanks to those I have been surrounded by over the years who have taught me valuable lessons including my parents, stepparents, siblings, and friends. Valuable lessons that I trust today to guide me well into the future and for future generations. They've taught me well. Whatever life gives me, I'm ready; and if I'm not, I'll figure it out.

Don't Miss Stop Signs or Exit Signs

I, middle-aged man, know that I must be aware of signs that are revealed when it's time to change the road I'm on. There are no awards for "hanging in there" while metaphorically going too far down the wrong road, or missing a turn-off when sign after sign is telling me to exit from the current road I'm traveling on.

Rowing the Boat

I, middle-aged man, should make sure everybody in my boat is rowing, not drilling holes in it when I'm not looking.

Don't Play Small

I, middle-aged man, am mindful of something that Nelson Mandela once said:

"There is no passion to be found playing small and settling for a life that's less than the one you're capable of living."

Quitting Something on Your Terms

I, middle-aged man, push myself. When I find myself unable to go any farther, to the point of wanting to quit, I don't quit the first time. I keep going a little farther. I don't even quit the second time. I go a little farther still. Give it three tries and then we will know it's the right time to give up on something or change paths on our terms. Quit too soon, and we'll wonder what if. Quit too late, and we'll lose the ability to stop doing whatever it is within our own power.

Take Care of Your Personal Affairs

I, middle-aged man, know that someday it will all end. Take care of the kids. Give them all that we had and didn't have. Create the foundations – emotional, physical and financial - for a better life for them. Everything and everyone else are just noise. You'll long be forgotten by most people, but family, kids and grandkids will be the ones who live with memories of us and what we leave behind.

Run **Into** the Storm

I, middle-aged man, follow certain metaphors in my own life. Specifically: hurricanes. Some people see a proverbial hurricane heading their direction and run away. They try and outrun the hurricane. It works for a little while, but eventually the hurricane is too powerful and has too much momentum, and it catches up to them. It engulfs and overwhelms the now-tired soul who has tried to outrun it.

Other people see a hurricane coming at them and they pause and collect themselves. Then, they head directly into the hurricane's path. They know that if they can reach the eye of the hurricane, they can take a breather, and then fight the 2nd half of it. The fast-moving hurricane passes by them, and they reach the other side. They are left weathered, battered and almost beaten down. But not defeated. They live to see many more days and are all the better for having run into the mighty hurricane - not away from it.

Inner Peace

I, middle-aged man, relish inner peace, contentment and pleasantness most. I wish to live my life in joy and peace, not chaos and drama.

Acknowledge People

I, middle-aged man, strive to always acknowledge people. It's the most basic form of respect we can offer someone, and we will have no regrets about doing so. We will never look back and have to say, "I wish I gave that person the time of day when I had the chance." Acknowledging others means providing a basic level of common decency and humanity in a world that is increasingly machine-like and too hurried to notice much of anything.

You're an Easy Target to Some

I, middle-aged man, am an easy target for some. Our successes to this point in our lives leave us vulnerable against those who chose different paths. Some of us have carved out relative importance in some areas of society, like civics, politics, athletics, business or entertainment. Others amongst us haven't found the levels of success that we have hoped for yet but are still young enough to act. No matter which group we find ourselves in, we are met with larger groups of people who think we have succeeded enough already or aren't meant to succeed more from this point forward. I, middle-aged man, vow to block out the noise, naysayers, and detractors and embrace the path that I see forward in self-actualizing.

Splurge on Travel

I, middle-aged man, vow to fly First Class whenever possible financially and logistically. The extra expense is real. The extra space, luxury and relative peace are also real. We recognize the need to splurge occasionally and treat ourselves well – or at least comfortably - in some areas of life, and travel is one of them. We recognize the need to not live life packed tightly like a sardine amongst the masses, and to break free from the pack. It's a gift to us to do this and should be the first choice whenever feasibly possible.

Be Proud, but Don't Boast

I, middle-aged man, vow to always remind myself where I came from, the journey to get here, and to allow pride to seep into my core. We recognize no one else at this stage of our lives will be a source of pointing out the good we've done, the obstacles we've overcome, the success we've earned, and the hard work physically and emotionally we've endured. It's up to us to provide our own best reminders of all this, hold it closely to our heart, and walk with an inner confidence each day.

Celebrate Improvements Around You

I, middle-aged man, vow to appreciate improvements in all things where we spot them. From physical structures to emotional growth in other people, we look outward at things, people and places that are going through the process of getting better.

What we see and appreciate outside ourselves we can then better internalize and apply to our own path of improvement.

We are a Small Part of All Things

I, middle-aged man, understand that we are part of something much, much bigger than ourselves. We are a part of an interrelated cosmos and universal energy that persists, and if channeled and manifested properly, assists us. We see in some people an inherent ease to life, devoid of the usual stressors that weigh down 99% of humans. We aim to function with a similar ease in our daily interactions with other people, within our profession, and in favor of our goals. We trust the universe will supply us with everything we need on whatever journeys we choose to pursue.

Let Go of One Thing Tying You Down

I, middle-aged man, vow to emotionally let go of one thing that we feel tied down by, or held captive by, today. We give ourselves permission to be free of things that weigh us down from being our best selves or becoming self-actualized. Instead, we're driven by the obligation we have to ourselves to live a life that's loving, fruitful and productive.

PART III: The Next Phase

*

For some of you who happen to be of a certain age, you know who "Mister Rogers" is. Fred Rogers. He's the man of "Won't you be my Neighbor?" fame. Regardless of whether you grew up watching the show or have ever watched any old re-runs, his life's work is something to be known about and studied. Some of my favorite words he ever uttered during an interview are reminders for us middle-aged men too:

The toughest thing is to love somebody who has done something mean to you. Especially when that somebody has been yourself. Have you ever done anything mean to yourself? Well, it's very important to look inside yourself and find that loving part of you. That's the part that you must take good care of and never be mean to. Because that's the part of you that allows you to love your neighbor, and your neighbor is anyone you happen to be with at any time of your life. Respecting and loving your neighbor can give everybody a good feeling.

His life's work was in helping kids. He was an expert at breaking down tough subjects for kids, and an expert on teaching kindness. He was all about care and compassion.

As a middle-aged man, those words above take on a new level of meaning, don't they? Read them one more time. How often have we beat ourselves up over bad decisions in the past? How often have we been unkind to ourselves or our neighbors for no real good reason? How often have we been perhaps not our best self and those around us suffered as a result?

I put this passage towards the end of this book for a reason. It's to leave you on a high note and highlight the kind of person we can all become. But how we treat others, and how others treat us, starts with how we treat ourselves. Give yourself a break. Mellow out a little bit. Take life seriously, but don't take yourself too seriously. How we carry ourselves and how we <u>feel</u> about ourselves takes the spotlight now.

You're here for a reason, and part of getting the most out of the rest of this journey is to foster that inner knowledge and confidence in yourself that your presence is enough. Are there things you can work on? Sure. Things you want to do better? Sure. But too often we look outside ourselves to improve on skills, talents, things or passion when we really should be honoring what's on the inside. We never get formally taught about how to improve the ways we treat ourselves. Now's your chance to self-instruct. Take it or not, it's your call.

*

Never stop trying to be the best you can be. Make it a goal to become self-actualized. That's under your control. If you get too distracted or wrapped up in things over which you have no control, you won't know your capacity or potential, much less reach it.

Don't listen to criticism. In fact, don't listen to too many people at all. If you do well, people will want to take you down a few pegs before you sail off into the sunset. If you don't do well, all you'll hear is the constant buzz in your ear by naysayers and told-you-so's. Keep a close circle of people you respect and can collaborate with as equals.

Do not let anyone talk down to you or diminish your accomplishments or who you are. You're too old to allow that.

Go against the grain occasionally. Better yet, plant your own grain.

Do what you believe are the right things unapologetically. Believe in who you have grown to be to this point and trust it. Other people might have different opinions than yours. Who cares? Get over it. Move on.

Continue to adapt to your surroundings and new situations, but don't lose your conviction. Don't get too high or too low emotionally. Stay even, stay low. Like that river we talked about.

Embrace and give gratitude to the good days. They always pass by quicker than you think. Wipe away the bad days just as quick. They too shall pass.

Best of luck to you throughout middle age. It's up to you to decide if it's a transcendent time in your life, or if it sucks like a lot of people say it does. My hope for you is that you find out it doesn't suck.

*

Author's Closing Meditation

What a few years. Middle age is hard.

While writing this book, I've gone through every life change imaginable it seems. I have an adorable new son, my 3rd child, to go along with my two amazing daughters. At present, I'm 49, so I'm not exactly winning any "young parent" awards at my kid's daycare. Before that, I found a woman whom I wanted to give family life another try with, which was frankly a minor miracle given the unpleasantness I had to live through in a past life.

I moved to a new town and into new home. I embarked on a new career, in what feels like it's now my hundredth. I lost my mom. I watched a long-time mentor and friend - my childhood tennis coach - pass away while sitting with him at his bedside. I went through early marital and parental adjustments of my own. I had some relationships and friendships get closer. I had some relationships and friendships get more distant. I met a lot of new people but spend time with only a few. I learned that most people reveal themselves when times are tough and when life is a little choppy. I learned that if I don't fit into other people's nice, neat box that they have constructed for me, I'll soon either become an outsider or people will get pissed. It's because the "me" they may have known from before doesn't really resemble the "me" today. And that's okay.

I experienced that there are some people who have problems with acceptance, of me, and my tendencies towards independence, quietness, my habits, or my shortcomings. In a major middle-age shift I've undergone, I'm much more determined in my beliefs and my life. Some people really don't like that and that's okay with me, too. I've got my own set of beliefs based on a smorgasbord of life experiences that have been incredible and exciting. I'm good with all of it.

I found out that as I weather the storms life throws at me and try and remain "even" - or stoic, as I say - emotionally, life continues to test me. We don't pass a test one day and be done. It's a test every day. It doesn't stop until it <u>all</u> stops.

I've felt sadness or disappointment at times. I've felt happiness a lot. I've kept a lot of my emotions to myself because that's how I process things and how I get through them…no one can do it for me, and in middle age, I don't feel it would be right to expect that anyway. I've learned – way before these past couple years actually – that there are caring people out there but that not every one of them must know my deepest, darkest secrets. I learned that all of it – every single component of life that I might see or judge as good or bad, challenging or easy, calm or irrational – is okay. I'll get through it.

I'm aware that in a blink it could all be over and won't matter much anyway. I learned that I must listen to myself, my heart and my most basic instincts first. I must trust my worth and my own intrinsic value. I must trust I've made it this far for a reason. I must trust that I'm never given hard things in life if I can't handle them. The Universe will always give me what I'm able to handle, never more than I can handle.

More so than at any other time in my life, I have a deep urge to continue to live a life that one day I can look back at and say the following about: "I treated my kids well, my spouse well, other people and friends generally well, was kind and generous, and sure got a lot out of life while I was here. I did a lot with life, and helped other people get through theirs maybe with just a little bit of added joy or assurance. And it's been one hell of a ride."

So, I, middle-aged man...

Have set and reached dreams, big dreams, sufficient my lifetime;

created new dreams;

failed;

created new ones;

failed;

reached a few big goals and made some dreams come true again;

failed hard, almost fatally;

reset what's important to me;

had some personal breakthroughs;

found true self-actualization;

took a step back again;

reached new goals again;

and then realized after all that that I'm just not the same person I used to be with the same perspectives I used to have. The old goals and old dreams don't work for the person that was left behind iterations and years ago. I'm still making new ones.

Footprints

Written: September 15, 2020, Fairfield, CT.

With every movement and step you take

There leaves an imprint, a shape, that's not a fake

Authentically yours, the prints stagger and sometimes weave

Often they're covered, but they never truly leave

From journeys that take you long and far

Maybe down a hill, over a horizon, or to gave at a star

Memories may fade but the marks that are left, stay

The signs of a life well-lived never go away

The things, the treasures, the pursuits all come and go

The real riches are found without searching for them high and low

As children, kids, and adults our form changes and morphs

But your essence always stays as you travel the course

You realize all the laughter, tears, joy and sorry are just a part

Of the great gifts that never really end, and often restart

How miraculous it is on that one day to look down and see

The tracks you're making right now blaze a trail for others to follow and be

Made in the USA
Coppell, TX
17 February 2024